Governance Beyond Borders

Governance Beyond Borders

Envisioning a Stateless Future

by
Ethan Ford Merkel

Ethan Ford MErkel

Copyright 2024 Ethan Ford Merkel. All Rights reserved. No part of this publication may be reproduced without consent of the author.

Governance Beyond Borders

Ethan Ford MErkel

Introduction

In an era of increasing global uncertainty, the traditional pillars of governance are showing cracks. From widespread political disillusionment to the rapid pace of technological change, our world is crying out for new approaches to collective decision-making. This book invites you on a journey to explore a radical reimagining of how we organize ourselves as a society.

Imagine a world where communities autonomously manage their affairs, free from the constraints of centralized authority. A world where emerging technologies empower individuals to actively participate in shaping their future. This isn't a far-fetched utopia, but a tangible possibility that's already taking root in pockets around the globe.

Throughout this book, we'll examine the concept of "post-policy" – a framework that moves beyond the rigid structures of traditional governance. We'll dive into the transformative potential of decentralization, exploring how it can foster accountability, diversity, and sustainability in ways that centralized systems often struggle to achieve.

But what do we mean by "governance" in this context? Far from the stuffy halls of bureaucracy, we're talking about the myriad ways communities can come together to make decisions, allocate resources, and solve problems collectively. From blockchain-enabled voting systems to innovative community models, we'll uncover the tools and strategies that are reshaping the landscape of human organization.

As we navigate these uncharted waters, we'll ground our exploration in real-world examples and relatable scenarios. You'll meet pioneers who are already implementing decentralized governance models, and we'll dissect both their successes and challenges. This isn't just an academic exercise – it's a practical guide for those who dare to envision and create a more collaborative future.

So, whether you're a disillusioned voter, a tech enthusiast, or simply someone who believes there must be a better way to organize our societies, this book is your invitation to think boldly about the future of governance. Let's challenge our assumptions, expand our horizons, and together, chart a course towards a more empowered and interconnected world.

Ethan Ford MErkel

Chapter 1: The End of the State as We Know It

Historical Context

The world of governance is always changing, much like the ground we walk on. It shifts in response to the flow of history, culture, and technology. To understand the big changes that lie ahead, we need to first look back at the origins of the nation-state system—a framework that has shaped international relations since the Treaty of Westphalia in 1648. This crucial agreement marked a significant shift in Europe's political landscape, bringing an end to the religious wars that had devastated the continent and introducing the idea of state sovereignty. This meant that nations could govern themselves without outside interference. The treaty laid down the foundations for concepts like territorial boundaries and legitimacy, which continue to influence our global system today.

As nations grew stronger and began to unify their power, they became the main players on the world stage. With the rise of the nation-state, the concept of citizenship changed, clearly defining the rights and responsibilities of people within these newly drawn borders. Nationalism emerged as a strong feeling, bringing people together around shared identities and common values. Flags flew proudly, anthems echoed, and borders were drawn with the ink of political ambition. What began as a way to resolve conflict turned into a tool for exclusion, as governments decided who belonged and who didn't. Citizens found themselves as both valued members of society and potential targets of state power, caught in a complex relationship that would shape the future for generations.

    Now, in our current times, the nation-state is facing a wave of challenges that threaten its very survival. Globalization has blurred the boundaries that once defined national sovereignty. Goods, services, and ideas now cross borders at lightning speed, making traditional state mechanisms seem less relevant. The rise of multinational corporations and international organizations has shifted power dynamics, creating a mix of authority that often exists outside the control of any single nation. In this landscape, the idea of a self-sufficient nation, with strict borders and a singular governing body, feels almost outdated—like a relic from a different time.

    Technological progress has also brought about a new era of hyper-connectivity. The digital age has not only changed how we communicate, but it has also transformed our ideas of community and belonging. Social media platforms allow people to connect across great distances, forming virtual communities dedicated to causes that go beyond geographic boundaries. The very makeup of societal organization is being redefined, as new networks emerge that favor collaborative governance over traditional hierarchies. This shift raises important questions about the role of the state: Can a nation-state still effectively serve its citizens when their loyalties might extend far beyond its borders?

Climate change poses another significant threat to the nation-state model. As rising sea levels and extreme weather increasingly force people from their homes, it becomes clear that environmental issues don't adhere to political borders. The challenges of climate change demand unprecedented cooperation among nations, highlighting that the world functions more like an interconnected system rather than isolated entities. Yet, how can we expect the nation-state system—often bogged down by nationalist rhetoric and self-interest—to respond effectively to these universal challenges? The limitations of state-centric approaches to global crises are becoming painfully obvious, urging a reconsideration of the authority and capabilities of current governance models.

Economic inequality adds another layer of complexity to this landscape. As wealth becomes concentrated in the hands of a few, the social contract that connects citizens to their governments starts to weaken. People everywhere are increasingly questioning how well their governments are addressing these growing disparities. In response, new models of governance are emerging, often from the grassroots level, as communities strive to regain control over their lives and resources. These initiatives—such as local cooperatives, decentralized support networks, and community-driven projects—

offer a glimpse into a future where governance may not necessarily align with the traditional state model. The desire for accountability and representation is prompting a reevaluation of power dynamics, challenging the long-standing hierarchies that have defined the relationship between governments and their citizens.

While the nation-state has been the primary framework for political authority for centuries, we now find ourselves asking: what comes next? The decline of state power is unlikely to happen overnight, nor will it be a simple process. Instead, it is expected to unfold through a series of intricate transitions, blending elements of continuity and change. Some nations may adopt decentralized governance models, paving new paths for citizen engagement and joint decision-making. Others may desperately cling to the existing order, resisting the historical currents that push them toward more inclusive and participatory structures.

In this rapidly changing global environment, the rise of decentralized governance models is not just a theoretical idea—it's a necessary response to the challenges facing the nation-state. Local communities may grow in importance as people seek to take charge in a world increasingly influenced by global forces. Technological advancements could empower citizens to engage in governance like never before. Imagine a world where blockchain technology supports transparent voting or where digital platforms connect citizens to collaboratively develop policies in real time. These innovations could transform power dynamics, leading to more equitable and inclusive governance that reflects the varied needs of the population.

It's important to recognize that the future of governance might not mean completely abandoning the nation-state. Instead, we may see a hybrid approach emerge, where decentralized systems work alongside traditional state structures. This blend could create new opportunities for governance that harness the strengths of both models. By promoting collaboration and accountability, such systems might develop a more resilient framework capable of tackling the complex challenges ahead. The ability to adapt to the diverse needs of communities could lead to sustainable governance that prioritizes the well-being of individuals over the mere pursuit of power.

As we reflect on the historical context that shapes our current political landscape, it becomes clear that the nation-state system stands at a critical juncture. The events of the 21st century have upended traditional ideas of authority, identity, and belonging, leaving us to consider what the future might bring. The path of governance is on the brink of transformation, inviting us to envision new possibilities that move beyond the limitations of current structures. During this time of uncertainty, individuals are called to engage—to participate in creating a society that mirrors their needs, hopes, and values in a fast-changing world. The end of the nation-state as we know it may not be an end at all; rather, it could mark the beginning of a new chapter in the ongoing story of how we govern ourselves.

Ethan Ford MErkel

Challenges Facing Nation-States

As we step into the age of globalization, we see its impact stretching far and wide, challenging the basic structures that support nation-states. Today's world is filled with new problems that make it even harder to govern effectively. For years, people have looked to nation-states as the main way to create political order, but now they face a host of challenges that are putting their authority and relevance to the test. It's clear that the stronghold of nation-states is being shaken by the very forces that were supposed to bring us closer together.

Globalization, with its fast pace and extensive reach, can feel like a mixed blessing. On one hand, it has connected economies, cultures, and communities like never before. On the other hand, it has weakened the control that governments have over their own territories. Just imagine an engineer in Silicon Valley who invents a groundbreaking technology that's made in factories in Vietnam, shipped to stores in Paris, and sold to people in Nigeria. This smooth flow of products and ideas is what globalization is all about. But as the lines between countries start to blur, the clear boundaries of authority and sovereignty also fade. What happens when decisions made in one part of the world send ripples across the globe, often disregarding national borders? The traditional idea of governing territory is in a tough spot, struggling with the reality that many issues can no longer be neatly contained within individual states.

Governance Beyond Borders

Migration is a powerful example of this struggle. As people cross borders in search of safety, work, or a better life, governments must deal with an influx of individuals whose hopes and needs often clash with political agendas. The European migration crisis in 2015 highlighted this issue, as thousands of refugees entered Europe, fleeing conflict and despair in their home countries. The reactions of different governments were strikingly different, revealing a mix of policies and attitudes that showcased the limits of conventional governing. Some leaders stepped up with humanitarian responses, while others turned to divisive rhetoric. This situation underscores a troubling reality: in a world where borders are increasingly open, the authority of nation-states to manage who comes and goes is being challenged.

Technological progress, while offering exciting possibilities, adds layers of complexity to governance. The rise of the internet and digital technologies has sped up change, giving individuals and communities the power to connect and organize beyond the usual boundaries of states. Social media platforms aren't just tools for chatting; they can spark movements that push against established power. A key example is the Arab Spring, when people across the Middle East and North Africa used social media to rally against oppressive governments. In that moment, the idea of nation-states was put to the test, as citizens seized the power of technology to demand accountability and change. The state, once the sole source of political power, found itself facing a reality where it no longer held all the cards.

Ethan Ford MErkel

When we think about the impacts of these technological changes, it becomes clear that the way we govern is shifting. Grassroots movements are popping up in response to government inefficiencies, often working outside traditional structures. Communities are finding their voices, and the ability to connect with others who share similar goals is leading to new forms of organization. Imagine a world where people band together, pooling their resources, embracing shared interests, and pushing for change without waiting for government permission. The rise of decentralized approaches shows an important truth: power is being spread out, and the grip of traditional governments is weakening.

Climate change is another major challenge that highlights the shortcomings of the nation-state model. The hard facts of global warming and environmental damage don't respect political boundaries; they represent a challenge we must tackle together. Rising sea levels, severe weather, and dwindling resources threaten to displace millions of people, pushing us to rethink how we govern. The 2015 Paris Agreement aimed to bring nations together to address climate change, but it quickly became clear that relying solely on nation-states was not enough, as some countries failed to meet their promises. The urgent need for climate action points to the importance of new governance structures that focus on cooperation, rather than competition, and that reach beyond the strict limits of national borders.

Amid these challenges, economic inequality stands out as a significant hurdle to effective governance. The growing divide between the wealthy elite and the struggling majority breeds distrust in government institutions, leading to social unrest and instability. As wealth gathers in the hands of a few, everyday citizens increasingly doubt their governments' ability to meet their needs. The 2011 Occupy Wall Street movement is a powerful example of this sentiment, as protesters rallied against the influence of corporate money in politics and the rising inequality that shaped the economy. This erosion of trust calls for a shift in how we think about economic governance, pushing us to look for new models that empower individuals and communities.

In response to these urgent challenges, fresh solutions are beginning to arise from the grassroots level. Community currencies, cooperative businesses, and local initiatives provide a glimpse into a future where governance doesn't have to follow the traditional state model. These decentralized methods allow individuals to take back control over their economic lives, creating systems tailored to local needs and shared interests. For instance, time banks—where people trade services based on time instead of money—help build community and support while reimagining what value and currency can mean. The rise of these initiatives shows a growing desire for accountability and representation, as communities work to reclaim control over their resources and futures.

The question of what lies ahead for governance is urgent, as the traditional nation-state model seems ill-prepared to handle the complexities of our modern world. We might start seeing a mix of decentralized governance models alongside the existing state structures, encouraging collaboration and inclusiveness. This blended approach could create a more resilient system to tackle the intricate challenges we face. The concept of power is evolving, with the potential to foster a fairer system that emphasizes cooperation and shared decision-making.

As we navigate the uncertain waters of the 21st century, it's vital that we engage in meaningful conversations about the future of governance. The challenges facing nation-states aren't just hurdles to climb over; they are deep chances to rethink how we govern ourselves. The future may not mean the end of the nation-state as we know it, but rather a reimagining of its role and authority in an increasingly interconnected world. The decline of the nation-state could mark the beginning of a new chapter—one where citizens actively shape their governance, where diverse voices are heard, and where working together leads to a sustainable and fair future.

In this complicated and interconnected age, the demand for innovative governance solutions is stronger than ever. It challenges us to envision a world where local communities gain importance, technology promotes transparency and accountability, and individuals are empowered to take on an active role in shaping what's next. The challenges before us offer a special opportunity to redefine what governance means, moving away from rigid territorial control toward systems that prioritize cooperation, sustainability, and inclusiveness. While the road ahead may be filled with questions, it's through these uncertainties that we can discover the potential for change, ultimately crafting a future that reflects our shared hopes and collective well-being.

Death Scenarios for the State

Imagine a world where the powerful institutions of government that once shaped our lives start to crumble, exposing the weaknesses in the foundations of state authority. The situations we might face are numerous and often troubling, ranging from a slow and steady decline to sudden and chaotic breakdowns. The idea of a state losing its grip on power isn't just a theory; it reflects real trends we can see happening around the world today.

The slow loss of state authority can feel like a leak that gradually turns into a flood. As people grow disenchanted, they disengage from traditional political systems, and the bonds that hold society together begin to weaken. This growing sense of discontent is something many of us can recognize today. More and more individuals are feeling disconnected from established political parties, leading them to search for alternative forms of governance. They are often looking for community-driven options that focus on local solutions instead of distant bureaucratic systems.

These local governance initiatives are born out of the needs and desires of communities responding to the shortcomings of traditional state structures. It's not that authority is completely gone; it's being redefined and reshaped. Picture a neighborhood council taking over responsibilities that were once managed by city government, handling everything from community gardens to safety programs. These grassroots efforts show a shift in the balance of power, illustrating how citizens can create new routes to self-determination when states start to lose their control.

Look at North America, for instance. Cities like Portland and Austin have seen a rise in local governance projects. Residents have taken charge, working on urban farming, waste management, and even local policing. In these cases, the state's role diminishes as communities step in to fill the gaps, coming up with solutions that fit their specific situations. The identity of the state is no longer a single entity; instead, it becomes a mix of local governance efforts that challenge the traditional way of doing things.

When states face crises—be they economic, political, or environmental—the threat of collapse can come suddenly and dramatically. History offers us a way to understand the potential for state failure. Countries like Somalia, devastated by civil war, have seen their traditional governing systems break down, replaced by clan-based organizations that stepped into the void. The once powerful state becomes a shadow of its former self, unable to withstand the chaos around it. In this situation, state power doesn't just weaken; it disappears entirely, giving rise to a new way of governing.

Economic downturns, from the Great Depression to the 2008 financial crisis, highlight just

Governance Beyond Borders

how fragile state authority can be. A sudden financial crash can spark widespread unrest and shake the very legitimacy of government institutions. Facing unemployment and losing trust in their leaders, citizens often look elsewhere for answers. This desperation can lead to protest movements, radical political ideas, or even the emergence of non-state groups that promise to restore order when the state has failed them.

Environmental disasters, which loom large in our minds today, also pose serious threats to state power. The growing effects of climate change—think hurricanes, floods, and wildfires—force governments to deal with challenges that go beyond borders. When disaster strikes, the immediate need for help can outpace bureaucratic processes, leading people to rely on grassroots organizations instead of the state. During Hurricane Katrina in 2005, for example, while government agencies struggled to respond efficiently, countless volunteers organized to provide food, shelter, and care for those affected. This situation not only highlights the state's shortcomings but also shows how alternative governance structures can emerge in times of crisis.

As we face the possibility of state collapse, it's essential to look at the innovative systems that might rise in its place. The rapid evolution of technology offers exciting tools for reshaping governance beyond traditional state structures. New models are beginning to take form, driven by advances in digital communication and organization. For example, Decentralized Autonomous Organizations (DAOs) use blockchain technology to enable governance without a central authority. These networks are built on principles like transparency, accountability, and participation, allowing communities to manage themselves without the constraints of traditional state oversight.

The promise of community-driven initiatives is immense. Many participatory governance models emphasize local decision-making and accountability. In places where state power has faded, local communities have stepped up to tackle issues from waste management to resource distribution. The success of these models shows a significant change in how we view governance—as a shared responsibility rather than something imposed from above.

Take rural areas as an example, where local residents come together to collaboratively manage resources. In India, the Mahatma Gandhi National Rural Employment Guarantee Act empowers rural communities to create their own job opportunities, fostering a spirit of agency and self-reliance. These initiatives not only meet immediate local needs but also help build a collective identity that goes beyond the limitations of centralized governance.

These examples point to a growing understanding that governance doesn't have to be restricted to the rigid borders of the nation-state. It can be flexible, adaptable, and deeply connected to the aspirations of the communities it serves. The power to shape governance can rest with those most affected by the issues, opening the door to innovative solutions that are relevant to their unique contexts and cultures.

Governance Beyond Borders

However, as we move forward, we must be aware of the challenges these decentralized systems can face. If we're not careful, alternative governance forms can create their own problems—like accountability, inclusiveness, and representation. While community-led initiatives hold great promise, they must be mindful not to reinforce existing inequalities or overlook vulnerable populations. The risk of exclusion reminds us of the importance of ongoing dialogue and a commitment to ensuring that every voice is heard in the governance process.

As we think about the future of governance, we need to recognize that the decline of state power isn't necessarily a bad thing. While it may indicate a loss of traditional authority, it also opens up opportunities to rethink governance models that focus on collaboration, diversity, and sustainability. The chance to create new paths for collective action, guided by the needs and aspirations of local communities, offers a hopeful outlook for what lies ahead.

Imagine a world where governance isn't defined by borders but by cooperative, innovative approaches, empowering individuals to actively shape their societies. By embracing technology and encouraging grassroots participation, we can create a future that prioritizes local decision-making and accountability.

The challenge before us is to critically assess the shortcomings of our current governance structures and envision a future where communities can flourish without the limitations imposed by traditional state dynamics. The decline of state power might not mark the end of governance; it could signal the start of a new chapter—one where diverse voices are celebrated and where collaborative efforts lead to sustainable solutions for the complex challenges we face.

In this exciting new world, the potential for decentralized governance sparkles on the horizon, inviting us to envision a society that embodies our shared hopes and well-being. It's a call to action, reminding us that the future isn't set in stone but is a canvas for us all to paint our ideas of what governance can be. The journey toward this future may be filled with challenges, but the opportunities ahead are rich with promise, encouraging us to move forward and embrace the changes that await us.

Chapter 2: Decentralization: Governance without Borders

Understanding Decentralization

To really understand decentralization, we first have to cut through some confusing terms that often pop up in discussions about this big change. Simply put, decentralization is all about spreading out power and responsibility away from a central authority. This shift can happen in various areas—politically, economically, and socially—leading to different interpretations and ways of implementing it.

Decentralized technologies, like blockchain and peer-to-peer networks, play a key role in this transformation. Unlike traditional systems that depend on a central authority to approve transactions and enforce rules, these technologies work on a network of connected computers that work together to keep everything running smoothly. This shift has huge implications for how we govern ourselves, as it allows power to be shared among many people rather than just a few.

At its heart, decentralization is built on values that celebrate independence and group decision-making. Autonomy means that people and communities can govern themselves, make choices, and act on their own without too much interference from central authorities. This idea aligns with the democratic belief that everyone should have the right to shape their own future.

Collective decision-making goes hand in hand with autonomy. It highlights the need for teamwork and consensus when making choices that impact the whole community. In this kind of environment, everyone's voice counts, fostering inclusivity and representation in how we govern ourselves. Essentially, decentralization creates a space where power dynamics shift, allowing individuals to actively participate in the decisions that affect their lives.

The reasons communities are moving towards decentralized models are as diverse as the communities themselves. Nowadays, there's a growing demand for transparency and accountability. Traditional government systems often face issues like corruption and inefficiency, leaving people feeling disconnected from their leaders. As citizens become frustrated with their governments, many are looking for decentralized options that promise greater involvement and oversight.

With the rise of the internet, we've entered an age where information is more accessible than ever. This change has sparked a desire for systems that reflect the same level of openness and clarity that people now expect in their everyday lives. The ability to track resources, confirm the legitimacy of decisions,

Governance Beyond Borders

and hold leaders accountable inspires communities to explore decentralized governance.

But we can't ignore the ethical issues that come with decentralization. The idea of spreading out power raises questions about fairness and access. While decentralization has the potential to empower people, it also brings challenges about who gets to participate. Not everyone has the same resources or knowledge to engage fully in decentralized systems, which raises the risk of creating new inequalities based on access to technology or information. Ensuring everyone can take part is vital for the growth of decentralized governance, and it requires thoughtful consideration from advocates of these changes.

Technology plays a crucial role in making decentralization possible. Advances in communication tools have changed how people connect, share information, and work together. Social media, for example, has helped grassroots movements gain traction and rally support like never before. In this evolving landscape, decentralized technologies can boost these efforts by providing secure, transparent, and reliable ways for communities to set up their governance frameworks.

Imagine a world where decisions affecting your community are made by the very people who will feel the impact of those decisions. This is what decentralization promises—a shift towards governance that is closely tied to the real lives of its members. In this new way of thinking, every voice counts, and everyone can play a part in looking after their shared future.

Ethan Ford MErkel

As we dig deeper into the idea of decentralization, it's clear that this movement is more than just a response to the shortcomings of traditional governance. It's a celebration of what people can achieve together. In a world that's changing rapidly, where we face more complex and intertwined challenges, having flexible governance is crucial. Decentralization encourages a diverse approach and supports the idea that solutions can come from the ground up, reflecting the unique needs of each community.

Centralized governance, with its top-down style, often struggles to effectively tackle local issues. On the other hand, decentralized systems are able to adapt their responses to fit the specific situations they encounter. This localized focus can lead to more effective and relevant solutions, as communities are in the best position to understand and solve their own unique problems. By tapping into local knowledge and promoting collaboration, decentralized governance can unleash the creativity and resourcefulness of its members.

Additionally, decentralized systems tend to be more resilient. Traditional governance structures can be fragile, especially during political upheavals, economic downturns, or natural disasters. In contrast, decentralized systems are inherently strong because their distributed nature allows them to adjust and respond to changing conditions. This ability to adapt is critical in times of uncertainty, where the power to pivot and innovate can mean the difference between thriving and struggling.

Governance Beyond Borders

As we look at different examples of decentralized governance—from age-old indigenous systems to the rise of Decentralized Autonomous Organizations (DAOs) in the digital space—we uncover a variety of ways communities have embraced this approach. Each case offers insights into both the possibilities and hurdles of decentralization.

The collaborative spirit of decentralized governance goes beyond just making decisions; it also builds a sense of community and shared responsibility. When individuals have a say in the governance process, they often feel more connected to their community. This sense of belonging can lead to increased civic involvement and a stronger commitment to the well-being of the community as a whole.

However, as we explore this exciting path, it's important to keep a critical perspective on decentralization. While there's a lot of potential for empowerment and innovation, there are also challenges that we need to address. We must be aware of the complexities of governance, the power dynamics at play, and the interaction between technology and ethics as we strive toward a fairer and more just future.

When thinking about the future of governance, it's hard not to wonder what a world dominated by decentralization might look like. How will traditional institutions adapt? What changes will occur in power dynamics, and what new forms of teamwork will arise? As we continue this exploration, it's important to remember that the journey toward decentralized governance isn't straightforward. It's a dynamic process shaped by many different voices and experiences.

As communities work through the challenges of governance in our connected world, decentralization shines as a hopeful option. It invites us to rethink the structures that shape our lives, inspiring us to embrace collaboration, accountability, and innovation. In this vision for the future, governance isn't something imposed from above; it's a collective effort rooted in the values of independence and shared responsibility.

As we move ahead, let's keep an open mind about what decentralization can offer us, recognizing the power that individuals and communities have to shape their own paths. In this exciting new landscape, the potential for meaningful change is within reach, waiting for those willing to tackle the challenges and seize the opportunities that lie ahead.

Case Studies in Decentralization

When we think about decentralization, it's one thing to talk about the ideas behind it, but it's a whole different story to see these ideas come to life. Over time, various communities, cultures, and even modern organizations have built their ways of governing around decentralized principles. By looking into these real-world examples, we can gain valuable insights into how these systems work, their benefits and drawbacks, and what they can teach us about governance in our ever-changing world.

Governance Beyond Borders

Let's start by taking a look at indigenous governance systems. Many indigenous groups around the world have thrived for centuries without a central authority. Their style of governance often revolves around shared leadership, making decisions together, and a deep connection to their land and communities. For example, the Iroquois Confederacy, a complex political system that began in the 12th century, united several tribes in what is now northeastern United States. Each tribe maintained its own governance while also participating in a larger council where important decisions affecting everyone were made collectively.

The Iroquois model stands out as a decentralized approach where power is spread out among different tribes instead of being held by a single ruling body. This system respected the unique differences among tribes while also promoting teamwork and mutual respect. The Great Law of Peace, which served as the foundation for the Iroquois Confederacy, emphasized unity, peace, and shared responsibility. In this setup, no one group held all the power, capturing the true spirit of decentralization.

We can see how this model impacts resilience and adaptability. The Iroquois Confederacy has lasted for centuries, proving that decentralized systems can handle challenges effectively. When faced with outside pressures, like colonialism, the Confederacy was able to adjust their strategies by relying on the collective input of their members rather than making unilateral decisions that could leave parts of the community feeling sidelined. This flexibility is a key benefit of decentralization, allowing communities to tailor their responses to specific situations in ways that top-down governance often cannot.

Now, looking at today's world, we see the rise of Decentralized Autonomous Organizations, or DAOs. These innovative entities mark a significant advancement in decentralization, powered by blockchain technology. A DAO operates mainly through computer code and smart contracts, allowing organizations to run without traditional hierarchical structures. In a DAO, members make decisions together, using tokens that give them voting rights in how the organization operates.

DAOs are transforming a wide range of sectors, including finance, entertainment, and social initiatives. One of the most famous DAOs, known simply as The DAO, was created to fund innovative projects. Members could propose ideas and vote on which projects to support. Even though it faced serious challenges—like a hack that resulted in significant financial losses—it sparked important conversations about the opportunities and risks that come with decentralized governance in our digital age.

DAOs show us a fresh perspective on how anyone can participate in decision-making, no matter where they are located. This opens doors to inclusivity and engagement, breaking down barriers that traditional organizations often put up. However, the lessons learned from DAOs also underscore the need for security, transparency, and a strong sense of ethics in decentralized governance—topics we'll dive deeper into as we look into various applications across different fields.

In finance, decentralized finance (DeFi) has emerged as one of the most thrilling uses of decentralization. DeFi aims to recreate traditional financial systems—like lending, borrowing, and trading—on the blockchain. By cutting out middlemen like banks, DeFi platforms enable individuals to access financial services directly. This shift not only makes services more accessible but also enhances transparency, allowing users to track and verify transactions on a public ledger.

A standout example is Uniswap, a decentralized exchange that lets users swap cryptocurrencies without relying on a centralized authority. Users contribute by adding tokens to liquidity pools, earning fees in return. This model not only democratizes finance but also encourages participation, as users have a stake in the system's success. By utilizing smart contracts, DeFi platforms foster an efficient, transparent, and inclusive financial environment.

However, while the allure of DeFi is strong, it also comes with its own risks. The lack of regulation, the possibility of smart contract vulnerabilities, and the complexity of the technology can make it challenging for newcomers. It's important to address these issues to ensure that decentralization in finance doesn't deepen existing inequalities or create new ones. This illustrates the need to balance innovation with caution, especially in critical areas like finance.

Ethan Ford MErkel

Education is another field where decentralization is making significant strides. Traditional education systems often face criticism for being inaccessible and not meeting the needs of all learners. Decentralized education is emerging as a promising alternative, using online platforms and community-led initiatives to create more equitable learning experiences.

Take Khan Academy, for example. This organization aims to provide free, high-quality education to anyone, anywhere. While it isn't fully decentralized, its model allows learners to access resources at their own pace and choose what they want to focus on. This approach reflects decentralized principles, empowering individuals to take charge of their education instead of following strict curriculums set by centralized institutions.

Additionally, platforms like Coursera and edX are further democratizing education by offering courses from universities around the globe. These platforms give learners the freedom to choose what, when, and how they learn, encouraging a sense of ownership and personal investment in their educational journeys.

Still, we need to remember the challenges that come with decentralized education. While these platforms provide valuable resources, not everyone has equal access to technology and the internet, which can worsen inequalities instead of helping to eliminate them. As we look into the potential of decentralization in education, we must make a dedicated effort to ensure that the benefits reach everyone, avoiding a situation where only those with technology privileges can succeed.

The world of community organizing also highlights the strength of decentralization. Grassroots movements have led the way in social changes for many years, often functioning without a central leader. When people come together around a common goal or vision, they can tap into the collective wisdom and strength of the community.

Nonetheless, the decentralized nature of these movements can create problems. Coordinating efforts among different chapters can be tricky, and differing priorities may sometimes lead to fragmentation. As we explore these movements, it's important to find the right balance between independence and unity, ensuring that decentralized efforts remain linked to a shared vision while respecting local identities and needs.

As we examine these case studies—indigenous governance systems, DAOs, decentralized finance, education, and community organizing—it becomes clear that decentralization offers a rich landscape to rethink how we govern ourselves. Each example shows the potential for more transparent, inclusive, and adaptable systems that elevate the voices of individuals and communities.

However, exploring decentralization isn't without its challenges. The very nature of decentralized systems raises important questions about accountability, inclusivity, and potential new forms of inequality. As we navigate this evolving landscape, it's crucial to carefully consider the implications of decentralization, making sure it empowers rather than marginalizes and promotes innovation rather than isolation.

In our quest for fairer governance, we need to keep the conversation going about the balance of power, the role of technology, and the ethical challenges that arise in decentralized systems. By learning from historical and modern examples of decentralization, we can gather valuable lessons that will guide us toward better ways of governing in our increasingly connected world.

The future of decentralized governance is still being written, but the opportunities are plentiful. As communities figure out new ways to organize themselves and their resources, we can only hope that the lessons from the past and present will lead us toward a more just and inclusive future. This journey may be complex, filled with its own set of challenges and barriers, but it's a journey worth taking—a journey toward a world where individuals and communities are empowered to shape their own futures.

Scalability of Decentralized Systems

The rise of decentralized systems has brought about a significant shift in how we think about governance and the structures that support these types of organizations. As people from all walks of life look for new ways to work together, the scalability of decentralized systems takes center stage. You might see scalability as just the ability to grow, but it's much deeper than that. It's a careful balancing act between broadening reach and keeping the core values of independence and teamwork that make decentralized systems so attractive in the first place.

At the core of scalability is the understanding that every community or organization has its own distinct needs, priorities, and identities. This is especially important in a decentralized model, where local independence is a fundamental principle. As networks grow, keeping this independence intact can be quite a challenge. This leads us to a crucial question: how do we foster collaboration while still respecting the unique characteristics of each part of the decentralized network? The answer lies in grasping the tools and methods that allow for effective communication, decision-making, and shared governance across a wider landscape.

A crucial part of scaling decentralized systems is creating effective communication channels. These channels function as the lifelines through which information flows, ensuring that ideas, concerns, and decisions are shared openly and efficiently. In traditional governance, information often trickles down from a central authority, leading to delays and misunderstandings. But decentralized networks flourish on real-time communication. Tools like instant messaging, social media, and video calls have become essential for keeping connections strong among members, no matter where they are located.

However, simply having the right tools isn't enough. It's about creating an atmosphere where open conversation is encouraged. In a sprawling decentralized system, different groups might have different viewpoints, and finding common ground can be tricky. It's important to cultivate a culture that values inclusivity and respect, where diverse voices are not just heard but cherished. Regular check-ins, feedback loops, and open forums can help members share their insights and experiences. By promoting a spirit of collaboration and engagement, decentralized organizations can more effectively navigate the challenges of scaling.

  Collaboration doesn't mean every decision must be made as a group, nor does it suggest a one-size-fits-all method. In fact, successful decentralized systems often tap into the strengths of local leaders who understand their communities' unique needs. These leaders can facilitate localized decision-making, allowing members to tackle their specific challenges while still contributing to the overall goals of the organization. This way, the specificities of local governance are respected while aligning with a shared vision that guides the decentralized network as a whole.

  Still, scaling comes with its own set of challenges, often pushing decentralized systems to grapple with the risk of fragmentation. As networks expand, the chance for miscommunication and differing priorities increases. In organizations where multiple groups operate independently, conflicting agendas can emerge quickly, leading to a loss of unity. It's crucial to find a balance between local independence and the overall objectives of the network. Regular communication, shared goals, and collaborative planning can help bridge this divide, ensuring that local needs are met while still aligning with the broader mission of the organization.

Technology plays an important role in the scalability of decentralized systems. Beyond communication tools, new technologies like blockchain provide a solid framework for decentralized governance. For example, smart contracts can automate procedures and ensure that agreements are followed without needing a central authority to oversee transactions. This level of transparency not only builds trust among members but also makes operations smoother as organizations grow. Plus, decentralized applications (dApps) can support innovative governance models, allowing for efficient resource use and member participation.

Despite the advantages, relying solely on technology can create new challenges. As systems get more complex, it becomes vital for members to have the technical skills to navigate these tools and understand the principles behind them. It's essential to empower participants with the knowledge they need to take an active role in shaping their communities' governance. Workshops, training sessions, and user-friendly resources can be valuable methods for creating a culture of learning within decentralized networks.

The issue of scalability also raises questions about the role of incentives in decentralized systems. How do we encourage participation and keep members engaged as networks grow? Incentive structures that reward contribution and involvement can motivate individuals to play an active role in governance. For instance, token economies can offer real rewards for those who put in time and effort into community initiatives. By acknowledging and celebrating contributions, organizations can build a sense of ownership and pride among members, ultimately developing a more resilient and active network.

As we think about the future of decentralized governance, we need to stay alert to the potential pitfalls that might come up during the scaling process. The risks of centralization can sneak in, often without us noticing. When certain voices consistently dominate discussions or decision-making, it can create an imbalance that undermines the very essence of decentralization. To counter this, establishing checks and balances is essential. This could involve rotating leadership roles, adopting consensus-based decision-making, or forming advisory councils that represent diverse interests within the network. By actively supporting democratic principles and valuing different perspectives, decentralized organizations can strengthen their structures against centralizing tendencies.

In addition to tackling power dynamics, accountability is another key consideration in the scalability of decentralized systems. As organizations grow, keeping transparency and ensuring that members are held accountable for their actions becomes even more important. Clear guidelines, performance metrics, and evaluation processes need to be in place to encourage responsible governance.

Governance Beyond Borders

Regular audits, peer reviews, and open discussions about performance can help uphold accountability standards while fostering an environment of trust and integrity.

The landscape of decentralized governance is constantly changing, influenced by the hopes and needs of its participants. As new networks pop up, so do fresh models for scaling. Some organizations are even trying out hybrid structures that blend decentralized and centralized elements, allowing them to use the strengths of both approaches. This flexibility makes it easier to adapt, ensuring that decentralized systems can effectively respond to shifting circumstances and community dynamics.

In the world of social movements, scalability often relies on collaboration among diverse groups with a common mission. While local chapters might operate independently, creating networks of solidarity can amplify voices and make a bigger impact. This interconnectedness not only strengthens individual organizations but also fosters a sense of belonging and shared purpose among members. The success of movements like Black Lives Matter highlights the power of collaboration in scaling decentralized efforts, showcasing how grassroots initiatives can drive broader social change.

As we consider the future of decentralized governance, the opportunities for scaling these systems are plentiful. By embracing technology, encouraging collaboration, and focusing on accountability, decentralized networks can widen their influence while staying true to their core values. The potential for innovation within these systems is boundless, with communities ready to reshape governance in ways that reflect their unique identities and aspirations.

However, with great opportunities come great responsibilities. Scaling decentralized systems requires a commitment to inclusivity, ethics, and social justice. We must ensure that as we build these networks, we do not inadvertently recreate existing inequalities or generate new forms of exclusion. The voices of marginalized communities should be elevated and prioritized, ensuring that all perspectives are included in decision-making.

As we navigate this complex landscape, keeping the conversation open and ongoing is critical. Scaling decentralized governance isn't a one-time job; it's a continuous journey that requires awareness, adaptation, and the willingness to learn from both successes and setbacks. By sharing experiences, exchanging ideas, and maintaining dialogue, communities can collectively forge a path forward that honors the principles of decentralization.

In a world that is becoming more interconnected, the lessons learned from the scalability of decentralized systems will be crucial in shaping the governance of tomorrow. As we deal with the complexities of modern society, we must stay committed to empowering individuals and communities. The journey toward decentralized governance is filled with challenges and opportunities, but it's a journey worth taking. By harnessing the power of decentralized systems, we can build a future where collaboration, independence, and inclusivity flourish—where everyone's voice matters, and governance is reimagined for the benefit of all.

Ethan Ford MErkel

> Governance Beyond Borders

Chapter 3: Power in the Networked World

Distributed Power

As we move through the exciting and often unpredictable landscape of the 21st century, our understanding of power is changing dramatically. Power, which used to be concentrated in the hands of governments, big companies, and influential people, is being transformed by the rise of decentralized networks. Picture a world where authority isn't just handed down from above, but flows freely among individuals and communities who work together to make decisions. This is the world we are starting to experience—one filled with distributed power.

The old way of governing, which often relies on strict hierarchies, is increasingly being questioned by new and collaborative approaches that encourage shared responsibility. In these new systems, power isn't something to be kept for oneself; it's something that is spread out among different groups and individuals. This shift towards decentralized power isn't just a theory—it's happening all around us, seen in grassroots movements and the rise of blockchain technology. Communities are using technology to create networks that amplify their voices and build trust. These networks aren't just tools; they're living, breathing entities that grow and change to meet the needs and hopes of the people involved.

Take, for instance, cooperatives like community-supported agriculture (CSA). In a CSA, farmers and consumers work hand in hand, creating a relationship that boosts local economies while reducing the risks of fluctuating food supplies. Here, power is shared evenly between those who produce food and those who consume it, fostering transparency and mutual support. This model stands in stark contrast to the traditional agribusiness approach, which often prioritizes profits over community well-being. The CSA model shows us a glimpse of what decentralized power can look like—a system where everyone has a stake, and together they create something even greater than what they could achieve alone.

We also see this idea in the growth of decentralized finance, or DeFi. This emerging sector, powered by blockchain technology, allows people to engage in financial activities without relying on traditional banks or financial institutions. In DeFi, individuals regain control over their money. Smart contracts help automate and enforce agreements, cutting out the need for a central authority and allowing for direct transactions between people. This innovation shakes up the established banking world, where power often rests with the institutions instead of the individuals they serve. By making finance more accessible, DeFi showcases how technology can promote distributed power.

Governance Beyond Borders

Trust is the key ingredient for decentralized networks to work effectively. Without trust, everything can fall apart. But how do we build and keep trust in a world filled with misinformation and doubt? The answer lies in being open and accountable. Many decentralized systems embrace transparency, enabling participants to hold each other responsible. For example, many blockchain networks use consensus algorithms that require agreement from the majority before any transactions are approved. This verification process fosters trust, as everyone knows no single person can manipulate the system to their advantage.

However, establishing trust in decentralized networks isn't always easy. Look at Wikipedia, for example. Its collaborative nature allows a vast amount of knowledge to be shared and added to, but it also opens the door to misinformation and bias. The very flexibility that makes Wikipedia a valuable resource can sometimes hurt its reliability. To address this, Wikipedia has put in place various editorial guidelines and community standards that stress the importance of using verifiable sources and maintaining neutrality. This ongoing effort shows that while decentralized power has the potential to empower, it also requires constant vigilance and a shared commitment to common values among those involved.

When we look at modern governance, the impact of distributed power is significant. Traditional government structures, with their rigid hierarchies, find it hard to handle the complicated challenges we face today. Problems like climate change, social inequality, and public health need a more cooperative approach that draws on the diverse experiences and resources of communities. A decentralized model allows for a richer understanding of these challenges, enabling everyone involved to come together and create solutions that are meaningful for their specific situations.

Plus, the democratization of power through decentralized governance models gives a voice to marginalized communities, allowing them to express their concerns and influence decisions. For example, in cities around the world, participatory budgeting allows residents to decide how public funds are spent. This change not only boosts civic engagement but also encourages a sense of ownership among community members. When people have a say in how their budgets are managed, they feel more connected to the outcomes of those decisions, reinforcing the social bonds that support healthy democracies.

That said, moving towards distributed power doesn't solve all our problems. The potential for new hierarchies to emerge within decentralized systems is something we need to watch closely. We've seen in various areas that power can still gather around influential individuals or groups who have the resources and charm to dominate conversations. For example, in the tech world, a few powerful social media companies can sway public opinion significantly. This brings up an important question: does decentralization really prevent the formation of oligarchies, or does it merely change how power is organized?

Governance Beyond Borders

To thoughtfully approach this question, we need to look at what motivates people to get involved in decentralized networks. Sometimes, the promise of sharing power can unintentionally lead to the concentration of influence among the most vocal or resourceful participants. This is particularly true in online communities, where early adopters or those with strong social connections can influence norms and decisions to benefit themselves. A good example is "influencer culture," where a small number of individuals with large followings can dictate trends and opinions in decentralized platforms. So, while decentralized governance structures have great potential, they are not immune to the same complexities and inequalities we've seen in traditional systems.

As we think about the effects of distributed power, it's clear that the road ahead is filled with both challenges and opportunities. The rise of decentralized networks invites us to rethink governance, focusing on cooperation and inclusivity. However, this transformation requires a commitment to building trust, transparency, and accountability among all participants. Creating resilient systems that can withstand outside pressures and manipulation is crucial. The journey toward a fairer distribution of power is ongoing and calls for everyone to engage, innovate, and hold each other accountable.

In this changing environment, the stakes are incredibly high. As we explore the possibilities of decentralized power, we must stay alert to the risks that come with any shift in authority. Understanding that power is not a fixed thing but a moving force that can be shaped by our collective actions is vital. The stories of community resilience, creative governance, and empowered individuals are just the start of a larger narrative that celebrates the potential of a connected world—one where power belongs to everyone, not just a select few. This evolving story encourages each of us to take an active role in reshaping our governance structures, igniting a movement of trust, teamwork, and shared responsibility. The journey is just taking off, and as we move ahead, we must believe that the future of governance is truly within our reach.

New Forms of Oligarchy?

As we journey through the twists and turns of our connected world, the idea of decentralization often shines brightly in front of us. It offers a chance to move away from the usual power structures—big corporations, bureaucratic governments, and long-standing institutions—toward a system where authority is shared more fairly, allowing the voices of individuals to rise above the noise of the status quo. But just like a double-edged sword, decentralization comes with its own risks that we need to pay close attention to. We should explore how these new systems can unintentionally create new kinds of oligarchies that mirror the very hierarchies they aim to break down.

Take a look at the tech industry, where a small number of companies have come to dominate their markets with an iron grip. Companies like Amazon, Google, Facebook, and Apple have gathered so much wealth and power that they can rival entire countries, raising alarms about how control has shifted. Their rise serves as a warning about the potential downsides of decentralized systems, especially when they become breeding grounds for monopolistic behavior. With so much power resting with just a few players, we need to ask ourselves: how does decentralization, which should promote fairness and inclusion, sometimes lead to a new kind of oligarchy?

The internet was once celebrated as the great equalizer, a place where anyone could share their thoughts and ideas without traditional gatekeepers standing in the way. Yet, as it has evolved, we've seen a few dominant players shape the digital space to their own liking. Consider social media platforms, for example. What began as open spaces for conversation has turned into tightly controlled environments where algorithms determine who gets seen and heard. This creates a cycle where those with big followings are further boosted, drowning out the unique voices of lesser-known users. The irony is striking: a medium meant to democratize communication has instead given rise to a new class of influencers, wielding power in a way that feels all too familiar.

The effects of this shift reach far beyond just social media. These companies have gathered enormous amounts of user data, giving them the ability to influence how we behave and what we prefer. Predicting and shaping trends is more than just a marketing strategy; it can have serious consequences for democracy itself. When a select few control the stories that dominate public discussions, it threatens the very essence of democracy. The idea of a well-informed electorate—critical for any democratic system—weakens when just a handful of entities control the flow of information.

As we look closer at the impact of these dynamics, we also need to consider how venture capital plays a role in amplifying these trends. The race for profits often results in an unyielding focus on growth and user acquisition. Startups are pushed to expand quickly, often sacrificing ethical considerations to gain market share. This creates an environment where innovative ideas can be swallowed up by a few monopolistic players, stifling competition and reducing diversity. The tech sector's obsession with disruption often leads to a buildup of power instead of the fair distribution that decentralization promises.

Let's also consider the financial sector, where blockchain technology was initially praised for its potential to democratize finance. Decentralized Finance (DeFi) sprang up as an ideal vision of a world free from banks and middlemen, but it has also shown troubling patterns. In many cases, those who got in early and had significant capital found ways to manipulate the systems to their benefit, leaving average users feeling left out. The promise of equality can quickly turn into a new kind of oligarchy, where only those with the resources to navigate these complicated systems enjoy the advantages.

Governance Beyond Borders

This issue isn't just confined to the private sector; it spills over into civic engagement too. In communities that have embraced decentralized decision-making, it can be all too easy for a vocal few to dominate conversations and decision-making. For instance, participatory budgeting initiatives can often fall prey to the very dynamics they aim to change. While these systems are designed to empower communities, those with the most time and resources tend to have their preferences prioritized, once again pushing marginalized voices to the sidelines.

The lessons we can take from these cautionary tales are numerous. First and foremost, we should recognize that decentralization isn't a cure-all for the inequalities that have long affected our societies. The same principles that help create inclusive systems can easily be twisted to create new hierarchies. As power shifts away from traditional institutions, we must stay alert about who is in charge within these new networks and how that power is being used.

Transparency, accountability, and inclusivity are crucial in fighting against the rise of oligarchies in decentralized systems. This means creating frameworks that guarantee everyone's voice is heard and that decision-making processes are open to scrutiny. In the tech world, open-source software and community governance models can promote collaboration and prevent power from becoming concentrated. Similarly, in civic engagement, fair representation must be a priority to ensure that those most affected by decisions have a say in what happens.

Ethan Ford MErkel

Furthermore, we should push for regulatory measures that tackle monopolistic behavior while still encouraging innovation. This is a tricky balance to achieve, as regulations need to be carefully designed so they don't stifle creativity and entrepreneurship. Policymakers should work closely with a range of stakeholders to come up with solutions that encourage resilience and fairness in decentralized systems. The goal should be to stop any one entity from becoming too powerful, ensuring that a variety of voices are present in all decision-making spaces.

As we think about the future of decentralized governance, it's important to keep a critical eye on the systems we create. We stand at a crossroads where the dreams of decentralization can either lead us to a world filled with equity and collaboration or pull us back into the familiar patterns of control and dominance. The stories of past mistakes and ongoing struggles remind us that we need to stay vigilant, as the road to progress often has its challenges.

The future is full of promise for a more equitable world, but achieving that vision depends on our shared commitment to building frameworks that encourage shared responsibility and accountability. The duty lies with each of us to engage actively with these systems, question who holds the power, and work together toward a more just distribution of authority. By nurturing a culture of openness and inclusivity, we can help ensure that the promise of decentralization doesn't lead to new oligarchies but instead fosters a vibrant networked society where every voice counts. In our quest for fair governance, we must remember that decentralization is not the final goal—it's a stepping stone toward a brighter, more democratic future.

AI as Arbiter

As we navigate the twists and turns of governance in a fast-changing world, it's becoming clear that artificial intelligence could play a key role in how we make decisions together. Just picture a future where AI isn't just a tool to make things run smoothly but becomes a vital part of how we govern ourselves in a more decentralized way. The possibility of making smarter decisions using data-driven insights is huge, but it also brings up a lot of ethical questions that we need to tackle directly.

Artificial intelligence is already part of our daily lives, influencing everything from the shopping suggestions we see online to the way our smartphones predict what we want to type next. But using AI in governance comes with its own set of challenges that need careful thought. What happens when we let algorithms make choices that impact people's lives? How do we make sure these algorithms don't carry biases? Will they just reinforce existing inequalities, or can they actually help us rise above them?

To start answering these questions, let's acknowledge that AI's ability to process large amounts of data can lead to better decision-making. Imagine a community facing an important decision, like how to allocate resources or improve public safety. An AI system could sift through tons of data—from demographic information to past outcomes—offering insights that human decision-makers might miss. This could lead to a governance model that goes beyond the limits of traditional bureaucracy. By using data, AI can help communities get a clearer understanding of their needs and make choices based on real evidence instead of just personal views.

However, as we welcome AI into the decision-making process, we can't ignore the concern of algorithmic bias. The algorithms driving AI systems are created using data, and if that data reflects societal biases, AI can end up making decisions that continue those biases. For example, if an algorithm learns from historical data that favors some demographics while leaving others out, the results can lean towards the majority. This raises a key question: how do we design AI systems that promote inclusivity instead of exclusion?

Openness is crucial here. In any governance model using AI, it's important that the decision-making processes are clear and accessible. Citizens should know how decisions are made, what data is being used, and how algorithms are being trained. This transparency acts as a necessary check against the often-concealed nature of technology, allowing those affected by decisions to hold the system accountable. Decisions that impact a community shouldn't just be left to a mysterious algorithm. It's vital to have human oversight, both as a safeguard and as a way to ensure that the community's voice is heard in its own governance.

Governance Beyond Borders

Finding the right mix between human judgment and AI-driven governance is a tricky balancing act. On one side, human intuition and emotional insight are essential for grasping the complexities of community needs. On the other side, AI can offer a level of accuracy and efficiency that people might find hard to match, especially in situations involving complicated data. The challenge is to weave AI into the decision-making process without letting it take over the human touch. Yes, AI can suggest options, analyze patterns, and predict possible outcomes, but the final decision should be made by individuals who are connected to the community and understand its specific context.

Moreover, the ethical dimensions of AI acting as a decision-maker extend beyond data biases. The way algorithms are crafted can reflect the values of their creators, often leading to unexpected results. If a governing body depends on AI to decide which projects get funding, the criteria built into the system might favor certain types of projects based on the values embedded in the algorithm. This raises another pressing question: whose values are we prioritizing, and how can we create systems that fairly represent a wide array of perspectives?

As we wrestle with these challenges, the idea of participatory governance becomes crucial. In a decentralized governance model, it's essential to involve a broad range of stakeholders in designing and implementing AI systems. This means including voices that are often left out of the decision-making process. By creating an inclusive environment where diverse viewpoints are welcomed, we can work towards AI systems that truly reflect the community's needs and aspirations.

In practice, this can look like many things: community meetings where residents share their hopes for AI in governance, workshops that explain how AI works and its potential impact, or collaborative efforts to create guidelines for ethical AI use in governance. These initiatives can help demystify AI, build trust, and empower communities to play an active role in shaping the technology that affects their lives.

Additionally, we need to set up accountability measures to make sure that AI used in governance doesn't lead to unexpected harm. This might mean forming independent oversight boards or ethics committees that examine AI decision-making processes. These groups could evaluate algorithms for bias, transparency, and ethical practices, providing an important layer of scrutiny that builds public trust in the systems in place.

As we develop these frameworks for AI governance, we must also remember that technology is always changing. AI doesn't remain the same; it grows and adapts over time. Therefore, the systems we create must be flexible and responsive to the evolving needs of the community and advancements in technology. Regular evaluations of AI's impact on decision-making will help ensure it continues to serve the public good while minimizing potential downsides.

The role of AI in decentralized governance also encourages us to rethink what accountability and responsibility mean. Traditional governance often places power in the hands of specific individuals or institutions. However, when AI systems enter the mix, accountability can become confusing. If an algorithm makes a decision that leads to negative results, who is responsible? Is it the developers who built the algorithm, the governing body that used it, or the community that chose to rely on it?

To navigate this complexity, we need to nurture a sense of shared responsibility. This means encouraging collaboration among technologists, policymakers, and community members to foster collective ownership of AI systems. When we see AI as a partner in governance rather than a replacement for human decision-making, it helps bridge the gap between technology and accountability.

Ultimately, our vision for AI as a decision-maker in decentralized governance is one where technology enhances human agency instead of diminishing it. AI has the potential to be a driving force for collaboration, enabling communities to tap into the power of data while staying true to their values and aspirations.

As we look toward the future, we need to stay alert in our quest for fair governance that emphasizes transparency, inclusivity, and accountability. The promise of AI in governance isn't just about making processes smoother or more efficient; it's a chance to redefine how we interact with each other as communities. By ensuring technology aligns with our shared goals, we can create a future where AI acts as a positive force, helping us make decisions that reflect the diverse needs of society.

This journey will require ongoing conversations, continual education, and a commitment to ethical values as we weave AI into our governance structures. As we aim to build a more responsive and fair society, the combination of human insight and artificial intelligence might just become the foundation of a new approach to governance—one that honors our collective voice while harnessing the power of modern technology. The path ahead may be filled with challenges, but it also holds incredible potential for creating a future where everyone has a say in shaping their own destiny.

By embracing the transformative possibilities of AI while staying rooted in ethical considerations, we can open up new paths for empowerment, teamwork, and community-driven decision-making. In doing so, we could not only change governance as we know it but also inspire a new generation of leaders who recognize the importance of using technology for the common good. The evolution of governance is underway, and with it comes the promise of a more inclusive and fair future powered by the synergy of human creativity and technological innovation.

Chapter 4: Digital Infrastructure for Post-State Societies

Blockchain and Governance

In the grand story of human civilization, where traditional governance has often been controlled by state actors, a new group of players is stepping into the spotlight on the digital stage. At the center of this change is blockchain technology—a groundbreaking force that has the potential to transform not only how we handle transactions but also how we govern ourselves. As we look ahead to a future that might break free from the old ways of state governance, grasping the role of blockchain is more than just an academic exercise; it's crucial for rethinking how power and accountability are structured.

Imagine a world where transparency isn't just a hope but a built-in part of our systems. Think about governance that extends beyond a top-down set of rules and regulations. With blockchain, we can bring this vision to life. The core of blockchain is its decentralized nature—data isn't stored in one spot but spread across a network of computers. This creates a record system that is nearly impossible to tamper with. Each transaction or decision gets recorded in chronological order within blocks, and when one block fills up, it connects to the previous blocks, forming a chain. This not only keeps the data secure but also makes it accessible to everyone in the network, encouraging an environment where transparency is the standard rather than the exception.

The impact on governance is remarkable. In a typical governance model, power often lies with a central authority, resulting in a lack of transparency and accountability. Citizens might feel powerless, frustrated by a system that seems to run without their input or oversight. Blockchain, however, turns this model upside down. It creates a participatory governance framework where people can get involved in decision-making directly. With tools like decentralized autonomous organizations (DAOs), communities can manage resources, vote on issues, and set norms without needing middlemen. This not only enriches democracy but also empowers individuals to take charge of their own governance.

The potential for increased citizen engagement is exciting. Consider the way we vote. In many places, worries about electoral fraud and disenfranchisement have long overshadowed democratic practices. Blockchain technology offers a way to move forward. By creating secure and transparent voting systems, citizens can cast their votes with confidence, knowing their voices are not only heard but also safeguarded from manipulation. Each vote could be recorded as an unchangeable entry in a public ledger, making it nearly impossible to change the results later. This enhanced integrity could restore trust in political systems, encouraging more people to participate who may have felt sidelined before.

Yet, while the promise of blockchain in governance shines bright, we also face challenges that we can't overlook. One major hurdle is scalability. As more people and organizations start using blockchain solutions, the technology needs to handle increased transaction volumes without losing speed or efficiency. Current public blockchains, like Ethereum, have faced criticism for being slow and expensive during busy times. Solutions like off-chain transactions and layer-two protocols are being looked at, but these also come with their own complexities. Striking a balance between decentralization, security, and scalability is an ongoing challenge that developers and communities need to approach carefully.

Equally important is the issue of digital literacy. While blockchain can empower individuals, it can also leave behind those who don't have the skills to engage with the technology. A significant portion of the population may find themselves unable to participate in blockchain-based governance if they don't understand how to use it. Closing this gap will be vital to ensuring that the benefits of decentralized governance reach everyone, rather than creating a new form of exclusion. Community education programs, engagement initiatives, and easy-to-use interfaces are all crucial for building a digitally literate public that feels confident in its ability to work with blockchain systems.

Another key factor is the legal and regulatory framework around blockchain technology. Governments are still trying to figure out how to classify and regulate cryptocurrencies and blockchain applications, which creates uncertainty that can hinder innovation. Finding a middle ground between promoting technological progress and protecting citizens from possible abuses is a delicate balancing act for policymakers. Clear legal frameworks that recognize the unique nature of blockchain can help reduce some of this uncertainty, paving the way for decentralized governance models to grow without unnecessary restrictions.

As we dive into these topics, it becomes clear that blockchain is not a magic solution that will fix all governance issues. Instead, it's a tool—an incredibly powerful one—that needs to be used thoughtfully. The potential for transforming governance is vast, but it requires a joint effort from technologists, policymakers, and citizens. By nurturing a spirit of collaboration, we can ensure that blockchain technology serves the public good, shaping a governance landscape that is more representative, fair, and sustainable.

The intersection of blockchain technology and governance signals a shift toward a more decentralized future, offering a new alternative to the traditional state-focused models that have shaped human society for centuries. It represents a profound change, where power is shared among individuals instead of concentrated in the hands of a few. This new system doesn't just tackle the weaknesses of current governance models; it also lays the groundwork for innovative approaches that respond to the needs and dreams of diverse communities.

As we think about the future, it's important to draw lessons from history. Societies have always adapted their governance structures to meet the changing dynamics of power, technology, and social organization. The rise of blockchain mirrors past movements that challenged the status quo and reshaped governance. From the signing of the Magna Carta to the rise of democratic movements, every shift has been marked by a fight for greater transparency, accountability, and citizen engagement. Blockchain is just the latest chapter in this ongoing story, and it holds the potential to rewrite the narrative.

What lessons can we take from these historical contexts? For one, the importance of inclusivity is vital. As we move toward a blockchain-based governance model, it's crucial that every voice is heard, especially those that have been left out in the past. The very nature of decentralized governance encourages participation from all corners of society, fostering dialogue and cooperation among a variety of stakeholders. This inclusivity can lead to richer, more informed decision-making processes that better reflect the richness of human experience.

Additionally, the success of blockchain in governance will depend on building trust. For people to engage meaningfully with these systems, they need to feel confident in their integrity and reliability. This trust isn't something we can take for granted; it needs to be nurtured through open processes, community involvement, and strong security measures. As we create digital governance frameworks, we must prioritize systems that build trust among participants, ensuring that our collective efforts in governance are based on mutual faith in the system.

In this evolving story, blockchain acts as both a spark and a canvas for new governance forms. It challenges us to rethink the very foundations of power and accountability, pushing us to create systems that are not just efficient but also fair and just. As we dig into the complexities of decentralized governance, we open the door to a future where individuals are not mere subjects of a state but active participants in shaping their own destinies.

The road ahead will undoubtedly come with its own set of complexities, challenges, and opportunities. However, with a strong commitment to working together, being transparent, and empowering each other, we can unlock the potential of blockchain technology to build governance systems that reflect the values and dreams of a society beyond traditional state structures. By doing this, we honor the legacy of those who have fought for greater democracy and accountability throughout history while paving the way for future generations to engage in a more participatory and fair governance landscape. The challenge is significant, but so too is the promise of a brighter, more inclusive future that awaits us.

Governance Beyond Borders

Smart Contracts and Autonomy

Imagine a world where the red tape of government fades away, replaced by a smooth web of automated agreements that make decision-making, resource distribution, and community involvement easier. At the center of this change is the idea of smart contracts—a groundbreaking tool that can transform how we think about and engage with governance. Unlike traditional contracts, which can be lengthy, filled with complicated legal terms, and often open to misinterpretation, smart contracts are straightforward lines of code that execute automatically when certain conditions are met. They are digital representations of agreements, and their ability to influence governance is significant.

To really grasp how smart contracts can shape governance, let's look at a few examples that show their flexibility and ability to make decision-making more democratic. One inspiring case comes from Zug, Switzerland, often dubbed "Crypto Valley." In this small city, local officials have brought in blockchain technology, including smart contracts, to simplify administrative tasks. Citizens can use these contracts to register businesses, pay taxes, and even vote on local matters. By taking advantage of blockchain's transparency and security, Zug has turned its governance model into one that is not only more efficient but also encourages active participation from its citizens. The outcome is a community where people feel they have a hand in shaping their environment through direct involvement in governance, fostering a real sense of ownership in local matters.

Another powerful example is the use of smart contracts in land registries. In countries like Georgia and Sweden, these contracts are being used to create unchangeable records of land ownership. This advancement not only cuts down on fraud but also speeds up property transactions. With a smart contract in place, once a buyer fulfills the conditions set out in the agreement—like transferring funds—the ownership of the property automatically updates in the digital registry. This process removes the long and often unclear steps that come with traditional land registries. Citizens engaging in the property market gain security and transparency, building trust in the system and encouraging more people to participate in buying and selling properties.

Yet, while these examples highlight the promise of smart contracts in governance, they also uncover some challenges we need to address. One major hurdle is the legal recognition of smart contracts, which is vital for their wider use. In many places, the existing legal frameworks aren't equipped to handle the specifics of digital agreements. This brings up important questions: Are smart contracts legally valid? How are disputes resolved? Can they fit within the current legal system? Until we find answers to these questions, it might be tough to implement smart contracts in governance effectively.

Adding to this complexity is the need for current legal systems to adapt to new technologies. Traditional contracts depend on human interpretation, negotiation, and enforcement—elements that smart contracts lack. This raises concerns about how we can keep governance based on automated agreements flexible enough to meet society's changing needs. Policymakers must find a careful balance, enjoying the advantages of automation while ensuring the system stays connected to human values and societal changes.

Beyond legal recognition, the flexibility of governance structures is another significant concern. Conventional governance models often depend on hierarchical authority, where elected representatives or appointed officials make decisions. In contrast, smart contracts promote direct citizen participation. This change requires a complete reevaluation of how we think about and carry out governance. Are we ready to accept a system where power is shared, and citizens can make decisions without intermediaries?

The possibilities of this shift are incredible. Picture a society where citizens can directly vote on policies or allocate resources via smart contracts, all while benefiting from transparency and security. This setup could lead to a more engaged and informed public, as people gain the tools to actively participate in governance. It might also create a culture of accountability, where decision-making is visible and can be verified.

However, it's important to acknowledge that not everyone will have the same access to these new technologies. The digital divide presents another challenge in effectively implementing smart contracts. In a world that increasingly depends on technology, those lacking digital skills or internet access may find themselves sidelined from governance. To ensure that smart contract technology is accessible to everyone, governments, organizations, and communities must work together to offer education, resources, and infrastructure.

As we look to the future of governance shaped by smart contracts, it becomes clear that a cooperative approach is crucial. Governments, technology experts, legal professionals, and citizens need to join forces to develop frameworks that support the use of smart contracts in governance. This teamwork should focus on establishing clear legal standards, promoting digital literacy among the public, and creating governance structures that can adapt to society's changing needs.

Another vital aspect of this collaboration is building public trust in the systems surrounding smart contracts. Trust is fundamental for effective governance, and for citizens to engage meaningfully, they must feel secure that these systems are reliable, fair, and transparent. Creating this trust involves being open about how smart contracts are designed and used and encouraging community members to have a say in shaping the rules that govern their application. Only through a participatory approach can we ensure that the advantages of smart contracts benefit all citizens, not just a privileged few.

Considering the broader implications of smart contracts in governance leads us to challenge the very ideas of authority and responsibility. In a world where automated agreements determine outcomes, what role do humans play? As we move toward a more decentralized and autonomous form of governance, we must confront how to maintain accountability in these systems. While smart contracts function based on set conditions, the ethical aspects of their implementation and the decisions made through them remain firmly in our hands. The challenge is to ensure that as we automate processes, we don't lose sight of our moral duty to hold ourselves accountable for the results produced.

Moreover, smart contracts can spark innovation in governance, inspiring entirely new ways to engage citizens and make decisions. By automating routine tasks, we can redirect resources typically spent on bureaucracy toward more complex issues that need human insight and creativity. This shift could lead to a governance approach that is more agile and responsive to community needs, encouraging experimentation and collaboration in policy-making.

Considering all these factors, it's obvious that the road ahead is not without its challenges. The potential of smart contracts to revolutionize governance is huge, offering possibilities that can improve transparency, security, and citizen participation. Yet, making this potential a reality will require tackling legal, technological, and social obstacles. It will take a commitment to inclusivity and cooperation, ensuring that all voices are heard in the discussion about the future of governance.

As we look to the future of governance powered by smart contracts, we find ourselves in a moment filled with both excitement and caution. The allure of an autonomous governance framework is tempting, but it calls us to approach it with careful consideration. The future will demand we be flexible, adaptable, and responsive to the needs of every citizen. If we can thoughtfully navigate the complexities of this transition, we might be on the verge of a new era of governance—one where citizens are empowered to shape their own futures through the incredible potential of technology. This journey is just starting, and as we move forward, it's crucial we learn from history while daring to imagine a future that is truly participatory, inclusive, and fair. The digital age gives us extraordinary chances to forge a new path in governance, one that champions autonomy and embraces the collective wisdom of the people. By harnessing the power of smart contracts, we have the opportunity to redefine what it means to govern and to create a society where every individual has a role in the decisions that affect their lives.

Security in Decentralized Systems

In a time when we often question and reshape traditional ideas of governance, the importance of security in decentralized systems has become a hot topic. The belief that safety and social order depend solely on state enforcement is quickly fading. As our societies grow and change, many communities are looking for new ways to ensure security that empower individuals and encourage shared responsibility. This new approach opens up exciting possibilities for how we handle safety, conflicts, and the dynamics of community life.

Community-driven projects and governance models are starting to take hold, proving that self-managed security can work really well and be sustainable too. The old top-down way of doing things, where law enforcement steps in as an outside authority, is facing challenges from grassroots movements that focus on local solutions. Rather than relying on distant government agencies, communities are taking charge of creating their own security systems. This change not only gives community members a sense of control but also builds an atmosphere of trust and teamwork.

One powerful example of community-led security is community policing. Unlike traditional policing, which often focuses on enforcement and punishment, community policing builds relationships between law enforcement and the communities they serve. This model encourages officers to connect with residents, understand their worries, and work together to solve problems. In this way, community policing becomes a vital part of decentralized security, promoting conversation and trust instead of fear and division.

Take, for instance, the neighborhood of West Seattle. Local residents got together to create a neighborhood watch program because they were worried about rising crime rates. They held meetings, set up ways to communicate, and formed a cooperative relationship with local police. Through this collaboration, residents learned how to report suspicious activities while also practicing restorative methods that focused on dialogue and reconciliation instead of punishment. As a result, the program not only reduced crime but also strengthened the community, showcasing the power of working together to promote safety.

Restorative justice practices also play a significant role in decentralized security by focusing on healing rather than punishment. This approach brings together everyone involved in a conflict—victims, offenders, and community members—for dialogue aimed at finding solutions and mending relationships. Instead of leaning on a punitive system that can leave individuals feeling isolated, restorative justice empowers communities to handle their own conflict resolution. By putting the needs and voices of those impacted at the forefront, this method fosters empathy and understanding, ultimately leading to better, more lasting outcomes.

A great illustration of restorative justice can be seen in Richmond, California. After dealing with significant violence and gang activity, local leaders decided to shift the focus away from punishment and move towards healing. They set up the Richmond Community Violence Prevention Program, which embraced restorative justice principles. This initiative brought together victims and offenders in structured discussions, allowing them to express their feelings, share their stories, and work towards mutual understanding. The results have been remarkable; by emphasizing healing and accountability, Richmond has experienced a noticeable drop in violence over the years, proving that effective conflict resolution can thrive in a decentralized setup.

Peer mediation is another creative approach communities are adopting to manage conflicts without needing state intervention. This method allows individuals to resolve their disputes themselves, with trained mediators helping to guide open communication and negotiation. By teaching community members conflict resolution skills, peer mediation nurtures a culture of collaboration and compassion. This decentralized tactic eases the strain on formal legal systems and reinforces community bonds, as people learn to handle their differences in constructive ways.

A notable instance of peer mediation appears in schools, where students are trained to mediate for their peers. In a program rolled out in several urban schools, students learn conflict resolution techniques and communication skills, enabling them to mediate disagreements among classmates. This initiative has resulted in a considerable decrease in suspensions and disciplinary actions, as students learn to tackle their conflicts before they escalate. By empowering young people to take the lead in resolving their own disputes, schools can create safer and more supportive environments, highlighting the potential of decentralized conflict management.

At the core of these examples is a shared theme: the importance of trust and teamwork in maintaining social harmony. In decentralized systems, individuals are motivated to take an active role in their community's safety and conflict resolution processes.

This collaborative approach builds trust among community members and reinforces the idea that everyone has a part to play in creating a safe and inclusive environment. As people get involved in collective security efforts, they develop a sense of responsibility for one another, leading to a more resilient community.

While traditional state enforcement often fosters distrust among marginalized communities, decentralized security models can help bridge this divide by prioritizing community involvement. This shift challenges the idea that safety rests solely on law enforcement and emphasizes that every individual has a role in ensuring their community's security. As trust grows between community members, so does their ability to work together to resolve conflicts and maintain social order.

Yet, moving towards decentralized security models does come with its own hurdles. Successfully implementing these systems calls for a cultural shift that values cooperation, empathy, and accountability. Communities need to create inclusive spaces where every voice is valued, especially those of marginalized individuals who have often been left out of decision-making processes. Achieving this inclusivity requires ongoing dialogue and education, along with dismantling systemic barriers that keep inequality in place.

As communities explore decentralized security mechanisms, they also need to think about how digital infrastructure can support these efforts. The rise of blockchain technology and decentralized networks presents exciting opportunities for enhancing community security. By providing transparent and secure platforms for recording agreements, sharing information, and facilitating transactions, blockchain can strengthen trust and accountability in decentralized systems.

Picture a community that sets up a decentralized platform for reporting and resolving conflicts. By using blockchain technology, residents can securely document disputes, share evidence, and track the resolution process. This transparency ensures that everyone involved is held accountable, while also giving them a sense of ownership over the conflict resolution process. The unchangeable nature of blockchain acts as a safeguard against manipulation, enabling communities to navigate disputes together and fairly.

Additionally, technology can improve communication and collaboration among community members. Social media platforms, messaging apps, and other digital tools can make it easier for individuals to share concerns, organize community meetings, and rally resources. By leveraging technology in decentralized security efforts, communities can overcome geographical barriers and create a sense of connection, even in an increasingly digital world.

However, we must be careful when integrating technology into decentralized security frameworks. Access and digital literacy are important issues that shouldn't be ignored. Communities without access to tech or the internet may find themselves further marginalized in conversations about security and conflict resolution. To ensure inclusivity, it is crucial to provide education, resources, and infrastructure that empower all community members to engage effectively in these processes.

As we imagine a future where decentralized governance grows, we must embrace the innovative potential of digital tools while making sure they are accessible to everyone. By nurturing trust, cooperation, and inclusion, communities can develop strong security mechanisms that reflect their values and priorities. The journey towards decentralized security isn't just about replacing traditional models; it's about redefining what safety and social order mean in ways that are participatory and fair.

In the end, the push for decentralized security is a call to empower ourselves. It invites us to rethink our connection with safety and recognize that we all play a role in building secure and supportive communities. By putting collective responsibility and community engagement at the forefront of conflict resolution, we can move towards a future where safety isn't something imposed from above but something we all cultivate together. This vision of decentralized security encourages us to embrace our shared humanity and invest in each other's well-being, creating a sense of belonging and solidarity that goes beyond the limits of traditional governance.

As we navigate the challenges of today's world, embracing decentralized security models offers a pathway toward a fairer and more equitable society.

Governance Beyond Borders

When we let communities take control of their safety and conflict resolution, we can foster a culture of collaboration, understanding, and resilience. In this vision, safety is not just about avoiding danger; it's about nurturing a vibrant and engaged community, where people unite to support one another in the pursuit of overall well-being. In this new world, the future of security rests not with a select few but with the hearts and minds of many.

Ethan Ford MErkel

Chapter 5: Culture, Identity, and Community in Stateless Futures

Post-State Identities

In our increasingly connected world, the idea of identity is changing in significant ways, often leaving behind the traditional concepts tied to nations. One fascinating example of this shift is the rise of digital nomadism. This movement invites us to look closely at how people create their identities and build communities in a space that knows no borders. As people explore various cultures and communities, the lines that once defined who we are are becoming less rigid. This opens the door to vibrant cultural exchanges, innovative social connections, and new ways of belonging that challenge old beliefs.

Digital nomads are a perfect illustration of this change. These individuals use technology to work from anywhere while traveling the globe. For them, the world isn't just a collection of places to visit; it's an exciting playground filled with opportunities for discovery and connection. This freedom to roam has a significant impact on how they form, adapt, and show their identities. Living and working in different environments encourages a fluid approach to identity, which stands in stark contrast to the fixed identities often tied to specific nations.

Ethan Ford MErkel

Traditionally, our identities might be shaped by our nationality, ethnicity, or the cultural symbols of where we were born. In contrast, digital nomads embrace a more flexible sense of self. They draw inspiration from the diverse cultures they experience, blending elements from each into their own stories. When settling in a new city or country, a digital nomad often dives into local traditions and languages, adjusting their identity to resonate with the spirit of their surroundings. This leads to an identity that is always evolving, changing with each new place they call home.

However, this journey of identity evolution is not without its difficulties. The nature of being a digital nomad often means that connections to local cultures are temporary. Although they may treasure the friendships formed in each new destination, the fleeting nature of their stay can lead to feelings of disconnection. To combat this, many nomads find camaraderie among fellow travelers, forming bonds with others who share similar lifestyles and dreams. In this way, digital nomads create a unique community that goes beyond physical borders, uniting people based on shared values and experiences rather than just postal codes.

Additionally, the growth of decentralized networks supports these new social connections. Platforms that connect digital nomads—like coworking spaces, online communities, and social media groups—provide opportunities for collaboration and cultural sharing. These tools allow individuals to exchange resources, seek guidance, and develop friendships that thrive beyond the limits of traditional state boundaries. As a result, the identity of the digital nomad becomes intertwined with a global community where experiences are shared, wisdom flows freely, and identities flourish.

The impact of these identity shifts goes beyond personal experience. This new form of global citizenship prompts us to rethink what community means in a world where traditional state affiliations are fading. As people increasingly define their sense of belonging through global networks, the definition of citizenship starts to evolve. What does it mean to belong to a community that includes people from every corner of the globe? This question is crucial as we navigate the complexities of identity in a world where state connections are no longer the main reference point for belonging.

One of the most exciting aspects of this change is the potential for rich cultural exchange. Digital nomads often act as cultural ambassadors, sharing their home culture with new communities while soaking up local customs in return. This two-way exchange fosters a vibrant mix of ideas, art, and practices, creating a colorful cultural landscape nourished by diversity. Instead of becoming a melting pot where unique cultures blend into one, the world may evolve into a mosaic where individual identities enhance one another, giving rise to new forms of expression and understanding.

As individuals break free from the confines of nation-states, they may also find new ways to challenge the traditional narratives of identity that have been imposed on them. In these decentralized environments, people are empowered to shape their identities on their own terms, liberated from the often-restrictive demands of national identities. This freedom can inspire a rethinking of personal and social identities, leading to views that are adaptable, inclusive, and affirming of varied experiences.

People thriving in this new landscape often embrace intersectionality, recognizing how different aspects of identity—like gender, race, class, and sexuality—interact and shape us. This deeper understanding encourages a more comprehensive approach to identity, acknowledging the complexities of human lives. In a world where traditional identities can clash, this perspective opens up opportunities for solidarity and mutual support among diverse communities.

Yet, the rise of post-state identities comes with its own set of challenges. While digital nomadism creates avenues for new experiences, it can also lead to feelings of dislocation. Maintaining meaningful relationships across distances can foster loneliness and isolation. What once felt liberating can sometimes seem like a double-edged sword; for every thrilling new destination, there's the inevitable goodbye to friends and familiar places left behind.

Despite this, there's a silver lining in this fluidity: the potential for resilience. The nomadic lifestyle encourages adaptability, allowing those who embrace it to develop a strong sense of agency over their own identities. They aren't tied down to a single story; instead, they weave their identities from a rich mix of influences, creating a unique patchwork that reflects their journey. This resilience can show up in various ways, from the quick ability to form connections to the capacity for self-reflection and personal growth in new surroundings.

The global pandemic has also accelerated changes in identity as people navigate a more decentralized world. Travel restrictions and the shift to remote work forced many to rethink their connections to places and identities. While some found themselves anchored in one location longer than expected, prompting a deeper bond with their surroundings, others turned to technology to connect with fellow nomads, nurturing relationships that might have otherwise faded.

As we reflect on these shifting identities, it's clear that the idea of belonging is transforming. No longer tied exclusively to nation-states, belonging can now emerge from shared values, goals, or experiences. Communities can form around common interests and aspirations rather than geographic closeness, allowing individuals to connect in ways that break the mold of traditional ties.

In this exciting new realm of post-state identities, the challenge lies in balancing the perks of global connectivity with the need for meaningful local involvement. While the idea of a worldwide community is captivating, we must not forget the significance of local context and cultural heritage. Individuals must learn to navigate the delicate balance between being part of a larger world while remaining grounded in their local environments, celebrating both their unique origins and expansive aspirations.

This interplay between the local and the global is especially important for cultural preservation. In a world marked by constant movement, it becomes vital to honor and uphold local traditions, customs, and languages while engaging with diverse influences. The challenge lies in crafting spaces where the richness of local cultures can thrive alongside the fluidity of global identities, ensuring connections that respect both the past and the present.

As we look ahead to a future shaped by these changes, the evolution of identity presents a rich landscape for exploration. The breakdown of traditional barriers invites new forms of belonging, encouraging individuals to engage with their identities in exciting and transformative ways. By embracing the complexities of post-state identities, we can nurture communities that are inclusive, resilient, and responsive to the diverse needs of those navigating an ever-changing world.

Ultimately, our journey into this decentralized future isn't just about losing the state; it's about reimagining what identity means. By welcoming the fluid nature of belonging, we can foster a sense of community that transcends borders, building connections that are both deep and transformative. As we navigate this new territory, it's important to pay attention to the nuances of identity, recognizing the power of diverse voices and experiences to create a world that celebrates the richness of human connection. In this exciting new paradigm, our identities can become the threads that weave together a vibrant, interconnected community of individuals exploring a stateless future.

Localized vs. Globalized Culture

In a time when the world feels more connected than ever, cultural dynamics are changing in exciting and complex ways. The relationship between localized and globalized culture often looks like a careful balancing act, where traditional practices are both cherished and challenged by the unstoppable wave of globalization. For generations, local communities have nurtured rich cultural heritages that shape their identities. But now, with technology and global connections transforming our lives, these local traditions are facing pressures like never before.

Take the lively markets of Marrakech, for instance, where the bright colors of spices mix with the joyful calls of street vendors. In this vibrant setting, local culture thrives, deeply rooted in the history and customs of the Moroccan people. However, the draw of global tourism brings in a stream of international visitors eager to experience this exotic place. While this surge can boost the local economy, it also raises an important question. Will the authentic experiences tied to local traditions bend under the weight of tourists' expectations? This is a vital concern for many communities, especially those that attract travelers.

It's not unusual for local customs to evolve in response to global influences. In various regions, traditional art forms have been reimagined, blending with contemporary practices to create something new and exciting. This mix of local and global can lead to stunning outcomes, showcasing a place's unique character in fresh ways. Yet, this blending can also spark worries about losing the essence of the original culture—the fear that in seeking global recognition, we might overlook what truly makes a culture special.

Cultural appropriation adds another layer of complexity to this conversation. Often, elements of local traditions are taken by those outside the culture, sometimes without genuinely understanding or respecting their importance. This can result in the commercialization of cultural symbols, reducing deep traditions to mere trends. For example, the growing popularity of yoga in the West has stirred discussions about its roots and the responsibilities of practitioners. What started as a profound philosophical tradition in India has been widely adapted and marketed to fit modern lifestyles, leading some to question whether its spiritual roots are being left behind.

Despite these challenges, there are inspiring stories that highlight the potential for peaceful cultural blending. The idea of "cultural blending" can be seen in places around the globe, where local and global influences come together to create something unique and authentic. Take New Orleans, a city where French, Spanish, African, and American cultural elements beautifully intertwine. The rich history is evident in everything from its music to its food, which has evolved into a celebrated mix of flavors and sounds. Jazz, born from various influences, shows how local creativity can flourish while embracing global beats.

Decentralized governance plays a key role in creating spaces where this kind of cultural blending can thrive. When communities have the freedom to make choices that resonate with their identity and values, they can develop policies that protect local traditions while also celebrating global influences. For example, cities that focus on cultural education and local arts can provide platforms for artists to share their work, ensuring that traditional forms are respected and preserved even as outside influences flow in.

Community-driven initiatives can also spark powerful cultural resilience. When local residents take the lead in promoting their heritage, they often discover innovative ways to share their stories with the world. Festivals celebrating local traditions, culinary fairs highlighting traditional recipes, and art exhibitions showcasing local talent all contribute to a lively cultural scene that thrives alongside global trends. These events not only boost local pride but also draw in visitors who appreciate genuine cultural experiences.

However, navigating this cultural landscape requires care. The relationship between globalization and local tradition is not a simple one. As communities welcome new influences, they must stay alert to preserve the core values and practices that define their identity. The challenge lies in making sure that local voices are heard in the cultural conversation, rather than letting outside forces set the terms for engagement.

One major concern about globalization is the risk of local languages and dialects fading away. As dominant languages—often English—become more prevalent in global communication, many local languages face the threat of extinction. Language is more than just a tool for communication; it carries culture, history, and identity. Efforts to revitalize and protect endangered languages are crucial in the fight against cultural uniformity. In places like Wales, revitalization programs have successfully breathed new life into the Welsh language, encouraging its use in schools and public life as a means of preserving national identity.

The digital age has also complicated the relationship between local and global culture. Social media platforms allow for the quick sharing of cultural practices and ideas, giving global audiences a chance to connect with local traditions. This can be a double-edged sword; while online content can highlight local culture, it can also oversimplify it into shareable snippets that lack context. For instance, the viral fame of a local dance can lead to its widespread imitation, but without understanding the cultural significance behind it, the dance risks losing its deeper meaning and community connection.

In many cases, cultural globalization has led to a blending of experiences, where unique local traits are overshadowed by global trends. Yet, within this reality lies an opportunity for creativity. The rise of hybrid cultural forms can spark new expressions that resonate with a wider audience while still honoring local traditions. Think of K-Pop, the South Korean music genre that has taken the world by storm. It skillfully combines local musical elements with global pop influences, resulting in a genre that is distinctly Korean yet universally appealing. This fusion has not only earned international acclaim but has also sparked a renewed appreciation for traditional Korean culture, demonstrating how globalization can indeed nurture cultural pride.

Moving forward requires a thoughtful understanding of the relationship between local and global cultural forces. Celebrating diversity must go hand in hand with protecting and preserving local identities. It's important for communities to engage in discussions about how globalization impacts their cultural practices while actively looking for ways to adapt to these changes. By creating spaces for cultural dialogue and exchange, we can foster an environment where local traditions thrive alongside global influences.

The role of education in cultural preservation cannot be overstated. Teaching younger generations about their heritage is essential to ensure that the spirit of local culture is passed down. Schools and community organizations can play a vital part in this effort, offering programs that celebrate local customs, languages, and traditions. When children learn about their cultural roots, they're more likely to develop pride in their identity and become guardians of their heritage.

Ethan Ford MErkel

Ultimately, the journey toward cultural coexistence is an ongoing process that needs collaboration, respect, and flexibility. The challenges brought on by globalization don't have to spell doom for local cultural traditions; instead, they can act as sparks for innovation, creativity, and resilience. By working together, communities can cultivate a rich cultural landscape that honors the past while embracing the future. It is this intricate dance between localized and globalized culture that will ultimately shape our collective identity in a world that keeps evolving.

As we explore this new cultural landscape, let's celebrate the richness of our diverse heritages while staying mindful of the dangers posed by uniformity. By nurturing curiosity and respect, we can build a world where local traditions thrive, global influences inspire us, and cultural identities become vibrant expressions of our shared humanity. In doing so, we embrace the full range of our experiences, weaving together a colorful mix of cultures that reflects the beauty of our interconnected lives.

New Citizenship Models

For a long time, the idea of citizenship has been closely linked to nation-states, defined by geography, political borders, and centralized control. But now, as the digital world seeps into our daily lives, we're starting to rethink what it really means to be part of a community. With new decentralized models

Governance Beyond Borders

and network-based identities, it's time to explore belonging in a different light.

Imagine a world where the strict lines that once defined citizenship—like those drawn on maps and stamped in passports—start to fade. This shift offers us a more flexible view of identity. It's not just a theory; it's becoming a reality thanks to advances in technology. With just a few taps on a device, people can connect with others around the world who share their interests and values, regardless of where they live. This change opens up exciting opportunities for both personal and collective empowerment, allowing everyone to take part in decision-making and governance in ways that suit them best.

Look at the grassroots movements that have sprung up globally. These citizen-led initiatives, fueled by social media, demonstrate the power of decentralized organizations that put community engagement first. People can share their ideas, voice their opinions, and influence their surroundings without needing traditional middlemen. It's a shift from being passive observers to active participants, where the way we govern starts to reflect what the people truly want.

Take, for instance, the local environmental initiatives that have emerged in response to climate change. Communities are coming together to create their own climate action plans, developing solutions that fit their specific situations. These grassroots efforts often grow organically and use decentralized tools that let people collaborate across different areas. They empower citizens to take control of their futures and foster a sense of ownership that goes beyond the constraints of traditional political systems. Here, citizenship is not just a label given by a government but a vibrant, evolving idea shaped by community involvement and shared responsibility.

However, as we step into this new era of citizenship, we must think about the effects on social unity and individual rights. With so many identities emerging, how do we ensure that people feel like they truly belong in their chosen communities? The challenge is to create an environment of inclusivity and respect that celebrates the diversity of identities while fostering a shared sense of purpose.

At the center of this discussion is the idea of decentralized governance. As traditional power structures become less dominant, new ways of governing are coming forward—ways that focus on shared responsibility and teamwork in decision-making. The big question is: how can these new models help people feel they belong while balancing their rights and duties as citizens?

One exciting option is the rise of decentralized autonomous organizations (DAOs). These groups use blockchain technology to create clear and fair decision-making processes. Within these organizations, individuals can take part in governance without a central authority, voting on initiatives that impact their communities. This democratization of governance not only empowers individuals but also creates accountability, since everyone has a stake in the outcomes of their decisions.

Governance Beyond Borders

DAOs are a perfect example of how technology can shake up traditional governance methods and open the door to new ways for citizens to engage. They represent a model of citizenship that values individual action while also highlighting the importance of working together. When people feel their contributions are acknowledged and appreciated, they're more likely to invest their hearts and minds in their communities.

As we think about these new citizenship models, we also need to consider the risk of social fragmentation. In a world where identity can be complex and fluid, how do we build a true sense of belonging to prevent feelings of isolation? The challenge is to find a balance between the many ways people express their identities and a shared commitment to the well-being of the community.

One effective approach is to create platforms that not only celebrate diversity but also encourage conversations among different identities. Programs that promote intercultural exchange—like dialogue initiatives, community events, and collaborative projects—can help bridge gaps between groups. By providing spaces for individuals to share their stories and experiences, we lay the foundation for empathy and understanding, reminding us of the connections that unite us all.

Education is also key in shaping these evolving citizenship models. As younger generations grow up in an increasingly decentralized world, it's crucial to give them the tools they need to navigate multiple identities while understanding their rights and responsibilities. Schools can promote a sense of global citizenship by focusing on critical thinking, cultural awareness, and civic engagement. By developing these skills, we empower individuals to actively participate in their communities, promoting inclusivity and cooperation in the face of division.

While we reflect on the future of citizenship in a decentralized world, we recognize that the evolution of identity and culture is an ongoing conversation. The balance between individual freedom and collective responsibility will help shape our communities. In this light, new citizenship models present opportunities for people to reclaim their voices, uplift their communities, and redefine what it truly means to belong.

Picture a future where citizenship goes beyond borders, allowing individuals to connect with multiple communities that reflect various parts of who they are. This future is closer than it may seem. It's already happening in many areas of life—from digital spaces where people gather around common interests to local cooperatives that promote sustainability and social justice. The possibilities are as varied as the people taking part in this change.

Still, as we welcome these new models of citizenship, we must keep a watchful eye on the rights of everyone involved. The advantages of decentralization come with the responsibility to ensure that marginalized voices aren't overshadowed amid the noise of differing identities. It's crucial to create inclusive decision-making processes that prioritize fairness and justice. Only then can we truly

Governance Beyond Borders

foster a sense of belonging that aligns with the principles of democracy and human rights.

The idea of a future without state boundaries—where citizenship isn't limited by geography—challenges us to rethink our understanding of identity and community. It encourages us to envision a world where individuals can shape their own paths and engage in governance that reflects their unique values and dreams. In this new way of thinking, citizenship transforms into a living, evolving concept that acknowledges the rich complexity of human experiences.

In this framework, our collective responsibility takes on new importance. As citizens embrace their many identities, the idea of being accountable to each other, to the community, and to our planet becomes even more significant. It prompts us to consider how our choices affect the wider network of relationships that define our lives. Through this lens, citizenship changes from a simple legal label into a deep commitment to our shared existence.

Looking ahead to a future filled with new citizenship models, we have every reason to be hopeful about the possibilities for creativity and collaboration. The issues we face today—climate change, social inequality, and political divisions—call for a united response rooted in shared values and mutual support. By embracing decentralized governance and inclusive citizenship, we can cultivate a spirit of cooperation that knows no boundaries and nurtures a true sense of belonging.

Ethan Ford MErkel

Ultimately, the journey of rethinking citizenship in a decentralized world is one of exploration and discovery. It invites us to reflect on who we are, challenge our assumptions, and connect with one another in meaningful ways. As we navigate this new territory, let's celebrate the richness of our diverse backgrounds while charting new paths of connection and teamwork. By doing this, we can create a future where citizenship captures the full range of human experience—one that values individual freedom, collective responsibility, and the lasting strength of community.

Chapter 6: The Future of Security, Justice, and Law

Restorative Justice and Peer Governance

At the heart of every society is a deep need for justice—a belief that wrongs will be righted, that people will be held responsible, and that healing can occur. Unfortunately, the typical view of justice often focuses on punishment and retaliation, which can create more problems than it solves. This approach frequently deepens divisions instead of bringing people together, making the issues at hand even more difficult to tackle. That's where the fresh idea of restorative justice comes in. This perspective shifts the focus from punishment to healing, along with the growing practice of peer governance, which brings community members into the justice process.

Restorative justice is based on the understanding that crime is not just a breach of the law; it's a harm done to people and relationships. This approach emphasizes the needs of victims, the responsibilities of those who commit offenses, and the role of the community in healing. Instead of seeing offenders merely as lawbreakers to be punished, restorative justice encourages everyone involved to

Ethan Ford MErkel

discuss the impact of the crime, promote accountability, and ultimately repair the damage done.

Key principles of restorative justice include accountability, open dialogue, and reintegrating offenders into society. Accountability here goes beyond just serving time or paying a fine; it means acknowledging the impact of one's actions and working to make things right. Dialogue is where healing happens—through guided conversations, both victims and offenders can share their feelings, experiences, and work together towards a solution that honors everyone's story. Reintegration is just as important; it recognizes that people who have made mistakes are still part of the community and can contribute positively when given the chance.

For centuries, indigenous communities have practiced restorative methods, offering valuable insights that can help shape modern justice approaches. Many Native American tribes, for example, have used communal circles for resolving conflicts, highlighting the need to restore harmony within their communities. These processes often include not just the offender and the victim but also family members, community leaders, and others, all collaborating to find ways to heal.

benefits of these community-centered models go beyond individual cases; they suggest a possible change in the entire justice system. As we look at the limits of state-run justice, it becomes clear that punitive measures often fail to address the root causes of crime. High rates of repeat offenses underscore this issue—when people leave traditional facilities, they often feel disconnected from their communities and lack the support they need to reintegrate successfully. On the other hand, restorative justice encourages a community ownership of the justice process, fostering collective responsibility that can lead to healthier social dynamics and lower crime rates.

Peer governance plays a crucial role in supporting these restorative practices. This term refers to systems where community members actively participate in maintaining order and resolving conflicts, rather than depending solely on state intervention. Involving peers in the justice process can create a culture of accountability and support, ensuring that offenders not only face the consequences of their actions but are also guided toward reintegration.

There are many ways to implement peer governance within restorative justice frameworks. Community-led initiatives, like neighborhood mediation programs or conflict resolution workshops, inspire local residents to actively engage in the justice process. These models allow communities to develop responses to conflicts that resonate with their values, making the outcomes more effective. Peers can mentor both victims and offenders, helping them navigate the emotional challenges of their situations and providing resources for healing and rehabilitation.

A great example of peer governance in action is the use of community circles, which have become popular in various regions for resolving conflicts. In a community circle, participants gather to share their views, feelings, and needs related to a specific issue. A neutral facilitator ensures that everyone has a chance to speak and be heard. This format not only promotes understanding but also encourages group brainstorming of solutions, leading to creative resolutions that may not arise in traditional court settings.

However, moving towards restorative justice and peer governance isn't without challenges. Critics often worry about the potential for power imbalances, especially if participants in the restorative process aren't on equal footing. There's a risk that the voices of marginalized individuals or groups could be overlooked in a peer governance setting. That's why it's important to put safeguards in place to make sure everyone can participate freely and fully in these restorative processes.

Additionally, successfully implementing restorative justice requires a cultural shift within communities. We need to move away from a mindset focused on punishment and embrace the principles of healing and accountability. This change means educating and reaching out to people to highlight the benefits of restorative practices, ensuring that everyone understands how these models work and why they're vital for creating a fairer society.

As we explore the impact of restorative justice, it becomes clear that embracing these community-focused approaches can lead to significant change. By prioritizing healing instead of punishment, we can create an environment where accountability goes hand in hand with compassion, relationships are mended, and communities thrive.

This shift could redefine our understanding of justice, leading to a more inclusive and effective way to resolve conflicts.

The principles of restorative justice and peer governance offer a fresh vision of safety and justice. They invite us to rethink our traditional views on crime and punishment and encourage communities to take an active role in promoting healing and accountability. Looking ahead, it's evident that the future of security, justice, and law may rest in the hands of the communities themselves, empowered to resolve their own conflicts and shape their own stories. This journey towards restorative practices is not just an evolution of justice; it's a call for all of us to step up as champions of healing, partnership, and solidarity.

Crime and Punishment without the State

In the ever-changing world of justice, it's natural to wonder: what happens when we remove the state, the traditional source of order and control, from the picture? This question is especially important today, as many of the old ideas about law and punishment are being questioned. Instead of depending only on state power, creative solutions for justice are beginning to sprout from the very communities that face crime. By looking at how technology intersects with community efforts, we can see that justice can thrive without a central authority. This shift could lead to a future where communities design their own systems for safety and security.

Ethan Ford MErkel

One of the most exciting developments is blockchain technology, which marks a significant change from traditional record-keeping. At its heart, blockchain acts as a permanent record—a digital ledger that can't be changed or erased without agreement from everyone involved. This unique aspect opens up new ways to improve transparency and trust in justice processes. Communities can document agreements, outcomes of restorative justice, and shared decisions in a way that builds mutual trust. Imagine a neighborhood where everyone understands the rules about criminal behavior and its repercussions, with community members able to see a clear record of actions taken and agreements made. Such a system not only promotes accountability but also reassures residents that their opinions matter.

Think about how blockchain could be used in restorative justice. This approach brings together victims, offenders, and community members to discuss the harm caused by a crime. By using blockchain, these conversations can be securely and transparently recorded, creating permanent records of the agreements made during the process. This is especially valuable in communities where there is a deep mistrust of authority figures. Being able to verify that an agreement has been made and followed can greatly improve the credibility of the restorative outcomes, giving everyone involved a sense of security.

The benefits of blockchain go beyond just keeping records; it could change how communities handle conflict. Picture a neighborhood that relies on a decentralized network to settle disputes through peer mediation instead of lengthy court cases. By allowing residents to vote on outcomes collectively and document the process on a blockchain, communities can promote a culture of shared responsibility and active involvement in the justice system. This change not only empowers individuals but also encourages a sense of ownership over the well-being of their community.

Still, the use of this technology comes with challenges. One major concern is access—who has the ability to use these blockchain systems? In communities with significant economic differences, it is crucial to ensure that everyone has access to technology and education. If only a small part of the community can engage with blockchain, then the aim of transparency and shared responsibility could fall short. Therefore, it's vital to develop inclusive frameworks that offer training and resources to all residents, making sure that everyone can benefit from blockchain technology.

Now let's turn our attention to grassroots initiatives, where community policing becomes very important. Around the world, citizens are stepping up to take control of their safety through initiatives like neighborhood watch programs and collective defense groups. These community-driven efforts show a growing understanding that residents are best equipped to tackle the unique challenges they face. Instead of waiting for state law enforcement to act, these programs encourage individuals to work together and take charge of their surroundings.

Ethan Ford MErkel

Neighborhood watch programs are among the most well-known examples of community policing. They encourage residents to stay alert and report any suspicious activity, fostering a sense of shared responsibility for safety. These initiatives also create lines of communication among neighbors, allowing them to share information and address concerns as a team. When a community stands together against crime, it sends a strong message: they won't tolerate wrongdoing and are ready to take action. This proactive approach is not just about watching; it's a way for the community to assert control in the face of potential threats.

Collective defense groups build on this idea, often forming in response to specific worries like rising crime or social unrest. These groups might come together to organize self-defense training, support vulnerable members of the community, or create safe spaces for discussion and conflict resolution. The focus here is on mutual aid and solidarity. Instead of relying on the state for protection, these communities actively work to shape their own security. They find ways to empower individuals and build resilience against outside threats, all without the presence of traditional law enforcement.

However, grassroots initiatives are not without their own challenges. Concerns about legitimacy and authority often pop up, especially when individuals take justice into their own hands. Who decides what behavior is acceptable? How do communities resolve disputes when disagreements occur within the group? These are crucial questions that need answers to maintain the integrity of community-led efforts. Building trust among participants and setting clear guidelines for how to engage is key to the success of these grassroots initiatives.

We can see many real-world examples of these community-based models in action. Across the United States, numerous neighborhood watch programs have successfully reduced crime rates. For instance, in a Chicago neighborhood that faced a surge in street violence, residents banded together to create a watch group. They organized regular patrols and set up a communication network to report incidents in real-time. Over time, their efforts paid off. Crime rates dropped, and a renewed sense of safety emerged within the community. This success story highlights the power of collective action and the impact that engaged citizens can have on their own security.

Likewise, in countries like Colombia, collective defense groups have formed in response to violence and civil unrest. These groups often consist of local residents determined to safeguard their neighborhoods amidst insecurity. By working together, they not only confront immediate threats but also push for broader social change, challenging the conditions that lead to violence. Their efforts demonstrate how community-led initiatives can transform not just safety but also the very structure of society.

Yet, while we explore these alternative models of justice, we must also be aware of the complexities that come with them. The lack of a central authority can lead to fragmentation and inconsistency in how justice is approached. Without proper guidelines, community initiatives risk sliding into vigilantism or exclusionary practices that push certain groups to the margins. Therefore, it's crucial to foster open dialogue that includes all voices in the pursuit of justice.

Looking ahead, the idea of voluntary courts and community defense networks offers another possible pathway for exploring justice outside of state control. These systems are built on cooperation and consent, allowing communities to create their own methods for resolving disputes. Voluntary courts operate on the principle that parties involved in a disagreement can agree to hand their case over to a panel of community members who will mediate and decide the matter. This model strongly aligns with restorative justice principles, promoting dialogue and collaboration to reach mutually satisfying outcomes.

Real-world examples of voluntary courts exist in many cultures. In some indigenous communities, traditional councils act as mediators for conflicts, relying on customary laws and practices. These councils have deep roots in their societies, allowing them to handle disputes in ways that align with local customs and values. This approach emphasizes that justice doesn't have to rigidly follow a legal framework; it can be a dynamic process that reflects the unique character of each community.

However, the success of voluntary courts depends on community members' willingness to engage with the process. Building trust in these systems is vital, as individuals must feel assured that their interests will be safeguarded, and that outcomes will be fair. This may involve education and outreach to ensure everyone understands how voluntary courts work and what benefits they can offer. Without this foundational work, the effectiveness of these systems could be jeopardized.

Furthermore, community defense networks can provide extra support when dealing with legal matters. These networks often consist of trained individuals who can offer guidance, resources, and advocacy for those facing conflicts. They act as a link between the community and the existing legal frameworks, helping individuals navigate the complexities of the system while encouraging them to take an active role in their defense. This dual approach—working within existing structures while also building community-led alternatives—provides a thorough response to justice that embraces both collaboration and empowerment.

Despite the promising nature of these alternative justice systems, challenges still exist. Questions of legitimacy and authority remain, especially when people choose to engage in community-led initiatives instead of traditional legal routes. Establishing clear engagement guidelines and addressing potential biases within community structures are crucial steps to ensure these models can thrive. Moreover, addressing access to resources—

both in terms of financial support and education—is essential for fostering a truly inclusive approach to justice.

As we think about crime and punishment without the state, it becomes increasingly evident that the future of justice rests in the hands of empowered communities. By harnessing individuals' collective strength, communities can create alternative systems that prioritize healing, accountability, and cooperation. Whether through the transparent power of blockchain, community policing efforts, or voluntary courts, the possibilities for justice beyond the state are not only innovative but also necessary in our ever-changing world.

Communities are not simply passive recipients of justice; they are active participants in shaping their own stories. While the path toward this decentralized model has its challenges, it is crucial for building resilience, solidarity, and ultimately justice that reflects the needs and values of the people it serves. In this new way of thinking, justice becomes a community effort, where every individual contributes to creating a safe and harmonious environment—one that thrives on collaboration instead of hierarchy. Thus, the future calls us to envision a world where justice is not an abstract concept controlled by the state but a vibrant, evolving process nurtured by the very fabric of community life.

Governance Beyond Borders

Conflict Resolution in Stateless Societies

In a world where we're increasingly questioning the institutions we rely on for sorting out disputes, a vital question arises: how do we handle conflicts in societies that lack a central government? Without a centralized authority, solving disagreements requires creative solutions that emphasize understanding and teamwork rather than adversarial stances. In these stateless settings, resolving conflicts is less about following strict legal guidelines and more about community-focused strategies that encourage empathy, open communication, and shared responsibility.

At the core of resolving conflicts in decentralized societies are a variety of practical tools and strategies that have grown directly from the communities themselves. Methods such as restorative circles, guided dialogues, and negotiation tactics have been developed to promote open discussion and create an environment of mutual respect. These approaches center on the needs and experiences of those involved, rather than on punitive responses. The spotlight shifts from assigning blame to seeking understanding, allowing people to dig into the roots of their disagreements and work toward lasting solutions.

One particularly effective method is the restorative circle. This approach gathers everyone impacted by a conflict—victims, offenders, and community members—into a safe space for conversation. The circle format encourages participants to share their experiences and feelings freely, without the fear of being judged. This open expression helps everyone recognize the impact of the conflict on their lives. As people begin to empathize with one another, they can collectively work towards an agreement that addresses the damage done and aims to mend relationships, fostering real healing instead of simply resolving the issue.

Facilitated dialogues represent another powerful approach in stateless societies. These discussions are led by a neutral facilitator who helps guide the conversation, ensuring all voices are acknowledged and respected. The facilitator's role is crucial in creating a positive atmosphere, encouraging participants to actively listen and respond genuinely. By promoting conversations that prioritize understanding, these dialogues can ease tensions, break down barriers, and ultimately lead to solutions that resonate with everyone involved. This method shows that conflicts can be resolved not through confrontation, but through cooperation.

Negotiation tactics also play a key role in addressing conflicts within decentralized communities. These communities can develop structured processes that allow individuals to express their needs while considering the viewpoints of others. Techniques like interest-based negotiation help parties identify the deeper needs behind their positions. This method shifts the focus from winning or losing to discovering common ground. By creating an environment where working together to solve problems is the goal, communities can come to agreements that are fair and just, addressing the root issues of conflict and paving the way for reconciliation.

The success of these community-led conflict resolution initiatives highlights how effective these collaborative techniques can be. In urban neighborhoods around the world, Community Mediation Centers have sprung up as grassroots solutions to local conflicts. These centers provide resources and trained mediators who assist individuals in resolving issues ranging from landlord-tenant disagreements to personal disputes. Having access to these services empowers residents to tackle their problems directly, avoiding the often adversarial legal systems that can heighten tensions and create more division.

Similarly, peer mediation programs in schools have become popular for teaching young people the skills needed to resolve conflicts. These programs train students to mediate for their peers, helping them navigate tensions that arise in their everyday lives. By encouraging a sense of responsibility and agency among students, these programs not only address immediate issues but also help to build a culture of empathy and understanding. The skills learned through peer mediation can leave a lasting impact, shaping how students approach conflicts throughout their lives.

The success of these community-driven initiatives emphasizes the need for reducing violence in conflicts. In a time when division and aggression often dominate discussions, these strategies highlight a more positive way forward. By promoting communication and empathy, communities can create spaces where conflicts are settled peacefully, which helps to avoid escalation and encourages healing. This focus on collaboration allows individuals to feel listened to and valued, reinforcing social bonds instead of tearing them apart.

Cultural aspects play a significant role in shaping how different societies resolve conflicts. Each community has its own unique traditions, values, and beliefs that affect their approach to disputes. Understanding these cultural factors is vital for crafting inclusive conflict resolution strategies that meet the specific needs and values of each community. By acknowledging and respecting various ways of handling conflict, societies can tailor their methods to develop solutions that are not only effective but also culturally appropriate.

For example, in some indigenous cultures, traditional conflict resolution practices often emphasize restorative methods that highlight community involvement and healing. Elders or respected members of the community might facilitate discussions, drawing on culturally specific techniques to help parties navigate their issues. These practices reflect the community's values and relationships, ensuring that resolutions resonate strongly with everyone involved.

In urban environments, however, there may be a greater mix of influences, as individuals from various backgrounds come together. Here, conflict resolution practices may need to adapt to fit the complexities of multicultural interactions. Developing a nuanced understanding of the cultural dynamics at play can lead to more effective mediation and negotiation processes, ensuring all voices are included and respected.

Beyond these practical tools, the larger themes of cooperation and mutual respect are crucial for fostering peaceful conflict resolution in stateless societies. Without the traditional institutional frameworks that often dictate how justice is delivered, communities must build their own norms and practices for resolving disputes. This shift requires a fundamental change in how individuals interact, emphasizing shared responsibility for the well-being of the community.

Communities that embrace these values are often better equipped to handle conflicts in ways that strengthen social ties. By prioritizing understanding, empathy, and respect, communities lay the groundwork for lasting relationships that can survive disagreements. As individuals learn to navigate their differences together, they reinforce the social fabric that holds them close.

Looking ahead, it's exciting to imagine a future where communities take charge of their own ways of dealing with conflict and justice. By creating systems that prioritize cooperation, understanding, and empathy, societies can build environments where individuals feel capable of settling their differences peacefully. This vision not only reflects a hopeful perspective on conflict but also acknowledges the immense potential of communities to shape their own futures.

Ethan Ford MErkel

In this future, individuals will actively engage in their own governance, taking responsibility for resolving conflicts within their communities. The absence of a centralized authority doesn't mean disorder; instead, it paves the way for creative solutions that reflect the unique spirit of each community. Human interaction flourishes when people are encouraged to engage in dialogue, creating an atmosphere where conflicts can be addressed constructively.

Ultimately, the pursuit of effective conflict resolution in stateless societies serves as a powerful reminder of the creativity and resilience found within communities. By focusing on understanding and cooperation, we can cultivate a future where disputes are resolved not by force or pressure, but by the collective strength and unity of individuals dedicated to forging a better world. The promise for peaceful coexistence lies within our communities, waiting to be realized through compassion, open dialogue, and shared goals. In this vision, conflict resolution becomes not just a necessity, but also a remarkable opportunity for growth and connection among individuals who are committed to nurturing the bonds that unify us.

Chapter 7: Ethical Dilemmas in a Decentralized World

Who Holds Accountability?

In a world that's becoming more decentralized, the question of accountability is becoming more important than ever. Our traditional governance systems are changing, and with this change, many people find themselves wondering, "Who is responsible for what?" The clear lines of authority that used to guide us are starting to blur, creating new challenges that make us rethink our understanding of accountability.

To really grasp what accountability means, we should begin by looking at its roots. In the past, accountability was pretty straightforward. You had clear leaders: an elected official was responsible to their voters, a board of directors answered to its shareholders, and government agencies had to follow the law. It was structured, and everyone knew what to expect. But as governance becomes more decentralized, where power is spread among various individuals and groups, those lines get fuzzy. Now, it's not just about figuring out who is responsible but also about how we make sure everyone shares that responsibility fairly.

Ethan Ford MErkel

Decentralized governance is often praised for giving power back to individuals and communities. It encourages people to take part in decision-making and work together without a central authority calling the shots. This shift towards shared power is exciting, but it also leads to tricky questions about who will keep one another accountable when traditional oversight is not present.

Take decentralized online platforms like blockchain networks, for example. These systems are celebrated for allowing people to make transactions directly with one another, bypassing the need for a middleman. While this can make things faster and cheaper, it also opens up a can of ethical worms. If something goes wrong—money disappears, a promised service isn't provided, or a scam happens—who can be called to account for it? Often, the answer is unclear. Without a central authority to turn to, people find themselves lost in a maze of responsibility, often feeling alone in these situations.

The need for accountability grows even more urgent when we think about the environmental and social effects of decentralized governance. Imagine a community that decides to handle its own waste disposal. Without a clear authority overseeing things, how can we guarantee that waste is managed responsibly? If a few individuals cut corners—like dumping trash illegally—who will face the consequences? In a traditional governance setup, rules would provide clear instructions and penalties. But in decentralized systems, it relies more on community norms and self-policing rather than strict laws.

Technology plays a dual role here, acting as both a potential hero and a source of complications. On one hand, tools like blockchain can improve transparency and traceability. Smart contracts can set up automatic agreements, making sure everyone does their part before anything changes hands. On the other hand, if these technologies are misused or misunderstood, accountability can become even murkier. The anonymity of cryptocurrencies can enable illegal activities, and the decentralized nature of these platforms can protect wrongdoers from facing consequences.

So, the real challenge is to build structures that not only encourage participation but also make accountability an integral part of decentralized systems. One way to do this is by creating community governance charters. These documents could lay out shared values, goals, and accountability methods, enabling individuals to hold each other responsible without needing a central authority. Such charters would have to be adaptable to fit the unique needs of different communities while still focusing on essential principles of responsibility and transparency.

Another powerful tool for boosting accountability in decentralized systems is participatory budgeting. This approach lets community members directly influence how resources are spent, which fosters a sense of ownership over community decisions. When people are involved in budgeting, they're more likely to hold each other accountable for the results of those choices. This practice not only encourages accountability but also strengthens community bonds as individuals gather to discuss and decide on shared priorities.

Moreover, by using technology to enhance transparency, we can close the gaps in accountability. Platforms that allow for real-time tracking of community projects can help reduce the risk of mismanagement. This tech setup makes it easier for community members to monitor progress, voice concerns, and celebrate successes together. When people have access to information, they can better hold themselves and each other accountable, strengthening the community's fabric.

These ideas become even more crucial when we think about how inequality plays a role in decentralized systems. While decentralization can lift up marginalized voices, it can also worsen existing gaps. In communities where knowledge, resources, or social capital vary widely, some individuals might dominate decision-making. That's why accountability measures need to be inclusive and actively work to address these disparities.

Picture a community where a handful of well-connected individuals control the direction of joint initiatives. If these individuals aren't held accountable, the projects may only reflect their interests and ignore the needs of others. This raises a big question: how can we make sure that decentralized governance stays fair, giving everyone a voice and a stake in decision-making?

One promising solution is to set up inclusive advisory councils that bring together various community views. These councils can act as a check on power, ensuring that decisions made in decentralized environments represent the wider community instead of just a small elite group. By promoting dialogue among different stakeholders, these councils can enhance transparency, boost accountability, and encourage a culture of shared responsibility.

As we look more closely at decentralized governance, it's clear that accountability isn't just about placing blame; it's about nurturing a sense of collective ownership. When communities recognize that they share responsibility for their outcomes, they open doors for active engagement and ethical practices.

The challenges we encounter are not just theoretical; they have real-world consequences that can influence how effective and sustainable decentralized governance systems are. The choices we make will determine whether these systems become places of empowerment and inclusion or slip into areas of unchecked power and inequality.

In this light, our task is to foster a culture of accountability that aligns with decentralized governance's core principles. We need to create spaces where individuals feel inspired to act and where collective responsibility is not merely an ideal but a reality they live every day. With innovative frameworks, inclusive practices, and solid technological solutions, we can develop communities that thrive on accountability, making sure that decentralized governance fulfills its promise.

As we navigate this new terrain, we must remain alert, questioning our beliefs and challenging the existing norms. By thoughtfully tackling the ethical issues surrounding accountability, we can harness decentralized governance to build vibrant, resilient communities ready to face future challenges. The future may be decentralized, but our dedication to accountability must stay strong.

Freedom vs. Regulation

In the ever-changing world of governance, the ideas of freedom and regulation often find themselves intertwined, sometimes harmonizing beautifully, but more often than not, stepping on each other's toes. This relationship is especially clear in decentralized systems, where the push for individual liberties can sometimes lead to chaos. Finding the right balance between freedom and regulation isn't just a theory; it's a real-life puzzle that affects people every day.

Picture a community coming together to create a cooperative business, pooling their resources to build something sustainable. At first, the excitement of operating independently is invigorating. Each person can share their unique skills and ideas, and without a central authority, creativity can thrive. However, without some level of regulation, this same freedom can lead to misunderstandings, unequal contributions, and ultimately, frustration. So, how can these decentralized groups keep individual expression alive while ensuring that everyone works together?

Let's look at the open-source software movement as an example. This movement is a

Governance Beyond Borders

fantastic showcase of decentralized governance in action. Programmers from all over the world join forces to create software that anyone can use, fostering a strong sense of community and shared purpose. The freedom to modify and share code allows for creativity without the limits of proprietary systems. But with this freedom comes the challenge of maintaining quality and security. How do these communities set standards without stifling creativity? The answer lies in a mix of self-regulation and collective responsibility.

Many open-source projects have governance models that include guidelines for contributions and a group of maintainers who oversee the project to ensure everyone's contributions align with its goals. This governance structure acts like a regulation but is based on community agreement rather than top-down authority. These maintainers don't just impose rules; they actively engage with contributors, offering feedback and creating a space where everyone can be heard. The outcome is a lively environment where innovation flourishes alongside a structure that keeps things on track.

Now, let's consider some environmental initiatives led by communities. Imagine a neighborhood taking charge of its waste management. On the surface, this is a beautiful example of local empowerment—people uniting to tackle a pressing issue. But without some form of regulation, things can quickly fall apart. What stops one neighbor from dumping hazardous materials in the local park because they think their freedom allows it? Here, community norms play a key role in setting expectations that protect everyone's interests.

These cooperative ventures and environmental projects reveal the delicate balancing act that decentralized governance must perform. They show that while individual freedom is a powerful engine for change, it needs to coexist with a framework of respect and shared responsibility. It's not just about avoiding chaos; it's about nurturing a culture where community members actively connect with one another, forming informal social contracts that, while not legally binding, carry immense significance.

Social contracts are the invisible threads that keep decentralized communities together. They emerge from the interactions among individuals, laying down expectations for behavior and accountability. These agreements might not be written down, but their impact is substantial. They foster a sense of belonging and shared purpose, reinforcing the idea that while people have the freedom to act, they also have a responsibility to consider how their actions affect others.

For example, in a decentralized community focused on sustainable living, members might agree to certain practices—like reducing waste or conserving resources—not just out of personal choice but because they recognize their interconnectedness. This creates a culture of accountability where actions are seen not just through the lens of individual benefit but in terms of community well-being. However, this system relies heavily on trust and communication, which can be fragile. What happens when someone breaks this social contract? The community needs to be ready to handle such situations, ideally through clear processes for resolving conflicts that emphasize fairness and equity.

Building a culture where freedom and regulation coexist smoothly isn't just a nice idea; it requires real actions and structures. Community meetings can be vital spaces for open dialogue, allowing individuals to share their concerns and hopes while together navigating the complexities of governance. These gatherings can spark innovation, where ideas are exchanged and solutions to pressing issues are developed collaboratively. Such participatory decision-making not only empowers individuals but also helps to create the social contracts that are essential to community life.

Having clear processes for conflict resolution is equally crucial. By establishing straightforward ways to address disputes, communities can ensure that individual rights are honored while prioritizing the group's well-being. This is a balancing act in itself—making sure regulations don't stifle freedom while still providing a framework for accountability. Think of it as a dance: the freedom of expression allows creativity to grow, while a solid partnership with regulation ensures that everyone is moving together.

The relationship between freedom and regulation is often messy. There will be disagreements, misunderstandings, and challenges that test the strength of the social contract. But it's in these challenges that communities can become more resilient. Embracing a mindset of adaptability allows decentralized systems to respond to new complexities. The ability to ask questions, engage in discussions, and revise agreements as circumstances shift is what keeps a vibrant and ethical community alive.

As we think about the future of decentralized governance, the discussion of freedom versus regulation becomes even more important. It pushes us to rethink our beliefs about individual rights and community responsibilities, encouraging us to find creative ways to ensure that both can coexist. Thriving communities don't succeed by getting rid of regulation; they do so by thoughtfully weaving it into the fabric of their governance.

Ultimately, the journey to balance freedom and regulation is not just about setting rules; it's about nurturing a culture of mutual respect, accountability, and active participation. By fostering this culture, decentralized governance can become a powerful force for innovation, empowerment, and social connection. The goal is not to eliminate regulations but to create a supportive structure that enhances individual freedoms for the sake of the greater good.

Navigating this complex dance may not always be easy, but it's this very complexity that makes decentralized governance so fascinating. As communities continue to explore the nuances of freedom and regulation, they will discover new pathways toward resilience and sustainability, shaping governance models that reflect their values and dreams. The challenge lies not in the divide between freedom and regulation but in weaving both together, creating communities where individuals can thrive alongside their neighbors.

The Problem of Inequality

When we look at the fast-changing world of decentralized governance, one big issue stands out like a beacon: inequality. While decentralized systems hold the promise of giving people more power and sparking innovation, they can also deepen the gap between those who have resources and those who don't. The contrast between inclusion and exclusion is very real, and as we discuss this important topic, we need to carefully consider how access to technology affects everyone.

The digital divide, a term that has popped up frequently in conversations about technology and fairness, is especially pressing when it comes to decentralized governance. Picture a world where everyone can take part in decision-making, where their opinions truly matter, and where resources are shared fairly. Unfortunately, this dream hinges on having access to technology and information. Without it, many people and communities risk being left out, with their needs overlooked or ignored. So, how do we make sure that the systems meant to empower everyone don't end up reinforcing existing inequalities?

To understand how serious this issue is, let's think about a small rural community trying to set up a solar energy project. Their goal is admirable—using the sun's energy to lessen dependence on fossil fuels and cut down on energy costs. But as we dig deeper into this situation, we see that not everyone has the same access to the necessary technology. Some residents might not have reliable internet, while others can't afford the initial costs of solar panels or their upkeep. What started as a hopeful dream of energy independence turns into a story of unequal access, leaving some residents struggling with rising energy bills while others enjoy the benefits of this renewable energy.

There are many real-life examples that show the stark differences between communities that have effectively addressed inequality and those that have not. Take, for instance, a bustling urban neighborhood that practices decentralized decision-making through community-driven projects. Here, residents cooperate, sharing resources and skills to create inclusive programs that tackle shared challenges. They set up mentorships connecting tech-savvy individuals with those who need help understanding new technologies. This proactive approach encourages collaboration and inclusion, making sure everyone feels like they have a say.

On the flip side, consider a community where technology access is limited due to economic conditions or geographical barriers. In these situations, the lack of inclusive systems often leads to feelings of powerlessness and disengagement. The voices of the marginalized can easily be muffled, stifling innovation. As decentralized governance aims to empower individuals, it can accidentally uphold a cycle of exclusion. To prevent this from happening, communities must focus on inclusivity and representation from the very beginning.

Focusing on inclusivity isn't just a nice idea; it's crucial for effective decentralized governance. When a variety of perspectives are involved in decision-making, the results are usually fairer and more meaningful. Recognizing this, we need to create frameworks that promote equity. This involves tackling the barriers that prevent access to technology, like investing in infrastructure to ensure reliable internet service in underserved areas.

Mentorship programs can be game-changers in closing this gap. Picture a situation where tech innovators team up with marginalized communities, sharing knowledge and resources. This mutually beneficial relationship can empower individuals to take charge of their own technological futures, creating a sense of agency that is vital for decentralized governance. When people from different backgrounds are encouraged to share their unique insights, the innovations that emerge are often more aligned with the community's real needs and desires.

As we delve into these frameworks, we must also think about the ethical implications of decentralized governance. At its heart, the issue of inequality leads us to confront questions about justice and fairness. How do we navigate the power dynamics in decentralized systems? When we set up governance structures, we need to think not just about who is included, but also about who is left out, and why. Those who already have advantages might unintentionally uphold systems that benefit them while sidelining those who are marginalized. Therefore, a commitment to equity should guide our efforts, ensuring that all community members are not just participants but active architects of their governance.

The digital age has brought us many technological advancements that, while exciting, also reveal weaknesses in decentralized governance. For example, blockchain technology promises transparency and accountability, but if it isn't rolled out carefully, it could worsen existing inequalities. As communities look to adopt such technologies, it's crucial to engage in meaningful discussions about who stands to gain from these innovations and how they can be used to uplift those who have often been overlooked.

Addressing the issue of inequality in decentralized governance also invites us to think about trust and communication. In a decentralized system, the connections among individuals form the backbone of the community. In tough times, it's this trust that helps everyone stand strong. But what happens when that trust breaks down? The answer can be troubling. Without solid communication and respect for one another, decentralized systems might fall apart. Building trust within the community requires openness, honesty, and a genuine effort to listen, especially to those who feel unheard for too long.

As we look for solutions, history can teach us valuable lessons. Many communities have stepped up, developing creative ways to tackle inequality. For example, some have created community networks—decentralized internet service providers built and run by the people who use them. These networks not only provide crucial connectivity but also reinvest their profits into local projects, creating a cycle of empowerment that uplifts everyone involved.

Furthermore, we can't overlook the importance of education. Giving people digital skills equips them to effectively navigate decentralized systems. Workshops, training sessions, and resources that simplify technology create a learning culture and encourage individuals to explore how they can positively impact their communities. By focusing on education, communities can build an environment where everyone has access to knowledge, allowing everyone to engage with and benefit from decentralized governance.

As we discuss these topics, it's important to remember that tackling inequality in decentralized governance isn't just a challenge to overcome—it's a chance to redefine what it means to be part of a community. By building inclusive frameworks from the start, we lay the groundwork for trust to grow and innovation to flourish. Every voice matters, and it's through the collective efforts of diverse individuals that we can achieve lasting change.

Moreover, as we continue to confront the issues of inequality, the moral obligation to address this problem becomes increasingly important. What kind of society do we want to create? Are we okay with letting technological progress repeat the same patterns of exclusion? How we answer these questions will shape the future of decentralized governance.

In our pursuit of more equitable systems, we need to stay adaptable. Inequality is a complicated issue that calls for ongoing conversations and reflection. The solutions we come up with today might need revisiting tomorrow, and that doesn't mean we've failed; it shows our commitment to continuous growth. Encouraging open discussions about equity helps create an atmosphere where everyone feels empowered to share their concerns and experiences.

Together, communities can forge paths toward inclusion, ensuring that the benefits of decentralized governance are enjoyed by everyone, not just a few. By recognizing potential challenges and suggesting real solutions, we can work toward a future where everyone has the chance to succeed, where their contributions are acknowledged, and where the systems we create reflect our shared values of justice and fairness.

As we find ourselves at the brink of this new era, the need to confront inequality in decentralized governance is clearer than ever. The road ahead may come with challenges, but it is also filled with opportunities. By embracing inclusivity and representation, we can pave the way for fairer governance models, enabling communities to shape their futures in ways that genuinely reflect their unique identities and goals. The pursuit of equity is not a final destination; it's an ongoing journey that requires dedication, teamwork, and creativity.

Together, we can create a new story—one that champions the principles of fairness, inclusion, and shared responsibility in the decentralized world we are about to enter.

Ethan Ford MErkel

Chapter 8: Imagining Governance as a Service

Subscription-Based Governance

In a world where we have endless choices—like picking a Netflix show or ordering a plant-based meal kit—why shouldn't governance work the same way? Imagine if people and communities could choose their own governance structures as easily as they select their favorite music playlists. This is the exciting idea behind governance as a service, which challenges the traditional ways we think about politics, civic involvement, and how communities make decisions together.

At its heart, governance as a service aims to reshape the connection between individuals and the systems that oversee them. Instead of a rigid structure that's imposed from above, this model focuses on giving people the freedom to engage in governance systems that reflect their values, needs, and dreams. This kind of flexibility could change governance from a burdensome obligation into an appealing option. But what does this look like in real life? Which current initiatives hint at this future, and what hurdles must we clear to make sure everyone is included and treated fairly?

To grasp this model, we can look at a few existing initiatives that showcase its principles. Cooperatives have long been a shining example of community-driven governance. In these setups, people come together to pool their resources and make collective decisions, showing how governance can emerge from shared interests and mutual benefits. For instance, local food cooperatives allow members to choose not only the products that are sold but also how profits are reinvested back into the community. This creates a governance system that's responsive and accountable to its members.

Decentralized autonomous organizations (DAOs) also offer a fascinating glimpse into governance as a service. These organizations use blockchain technology to let members vote on proposals and allocate resources in a transparent and democratic way. In a DAO, every member's voice matters, providing a fair platform for decision-making that's often missing in traditional governance setups. This model challenges the idea of top-down authority and encourages everyone to actively participate in governance.

However, while the idea of subscription-based governance sounds appealing, we need to be cautious. The benefits of personalization and responsiveness come with the risk of leaving some people out. If individuals can simply pick their governance framework, what happens to those who can't access these options? Will wealthier communities create systems just for themselves, pushing marginalized groups further to the side? The key challenge is to ensure that every citizen can fully participate in this new way of governing, no matter their background or financial situation.

Additionally, the risk of fragmentation raises concerns about how society can stay united. If people choose different governance models, how can communities keep a shared identity and purpose? There's a danger that governance as a service could lead to a mix of competing systems, isolating groups in their own frameworks and widening social divides. Finding a balance between personalized governance and community cohesion will be crucial if we want to enjoy the benefits of this innovative approach.

Another important thing to consider is the challenge of navigating multiple governance frameworks. In a world where people can choose from various systems, it becomes vital to understand what those choices mean. As consumers of governance, individuals might need to learn more about different governance models to make informed decisions on which systems match their beliefs. This responsibility for understanding and getting involved might create barriers for some, making the landscape of governance as a service even more complicated.

Still, there's a lot we can learn from models of governance that focus on community involvement and individual choice. Initiatives that stress cooperative governance not only empower individuals but also build a sense of belonging and shared responsibility. They encourage participants to engage with one another actively, fostering a collaborative spirit that can strengthen community bonds.

The promise of governance as a service is not just in its ability to personalize but also in its potential to motivate more people to participate in civic life.

Ethan Ford MErkel

When individuals feel they have a say in shaping their governance, they are more likely to get involved in political matters, advocate for their beliefs, and hold leaders accountable. This increased engagement can lead to meaningful change, as communities push for governance that truly reflects their shared values and goals.

Ultimately, the idea of governance as a service urges us to rethink our relationship with authority. It challenges us to reflect on the systems that govern us and ask whether they really meet our needs. In a world filled with complexity and diversity, this model could pave the way for more responsive and accountable governance structures that genuinely align with the dreams of the communities they serve.

As we look ahead to the future of governance through this lens, it's crucial to stay aware of the challenges that might come our way. The path to implementing such a model won't be easy, but by learning from existing examples and prioritizing inclusivity, we can work towards a future where governance feels like a service—something chosen by the people, for the people. Through this perspective, we can start to explore the bigger implications of governance as a marketplace, considering how competition among diverse systems could inspire innovation and adaptability.

In short, subscription-based governance opens up a fresh way of thinking about power and authority, one that invites individuals to take an active role in shaping their societies. Whether through cooperatives, DAOs, or other emerging models, the chance for a more personalized, accountable, and inclusive governance framework is closer than ever. By embracing this vision and addressing its challenges, we can head toward a future where governance is not just a top-down rule but a lively, collaborative service that evolves with the communities it supports.

Competing Governance Systems

Picture a lively marketplace, not filled with vendors selling fruits or handmade crafts, but a vibrant mix of governance models all vying for the attention of the public. In this bustling space, individuals and communities aren't just passive recipients of a single system; they're active participants in choosing the governance framework that best fits their values and dreams. This idea of a marketplace for governance, where different systems exist and innovate, is both exciting and complicated. It makes us think about how choice and competition can breathe new life into the often stagnant world of political governance, much like what we see in technology and education.

Today's world is full of examples that show how competition can spark innovation. Just as tech companies tirelessly work to create better software and devices, governance systems can learn and adapt based on what the citizens need and want. Think about it: if we have a variety of options for education—like public schools, charter schools, and online learning—why not extend that concept to governance? Instead of sticking to a single model shaped by geography or history, communities could explore many different approaches, each highlighting its own strengths and weaknesses.

This competitive governance could lead to a flowering of fresh ideas. When various systems live side by side, they can learn from one another, creating an atmosphere where innovation thrives. For example, a district might adopt a more transparent budgeting process after seeing how well a neighboring area's participatory budgeting model works. Or perhaps a community known for its high level of civic engagement inspires others to implement similar initiatives, raising the overall standard of governance. In a scenario where governance is treated like a service, the dynamics of the marketplace could push improvements in efficiency, accountability, and responsiveness, just like businesses do to meet customer demands.

However, it's crucial to look at real-life examples that show these dynamics in action. Take the city of Porto Alegre in Brazil, for instance, where they've been using a participatory budgeting model since the late 1980s. In this setup, residents can directly influence how the municipal budget is spent, leading to better infrastructure, social services, and community involvement. The success of participatory budgeting in Porto Alegre has inspired numerous other cities around the world to adopt similar approaches, each adjusting the model to fit local needs. This is a prime example of how one innovative governance system can create a ripple effect,

Governance Beyond Borders

encouraging other communities to rethink their governance structures.

Another interesting case is Estonia, especially with their e-governance initiatives. The country has embraced digital solutions that empower its citizens to engage more easily with government services, from online voting to streamlined business registrations. By focusing on transparency and accessibility, Estonia has set a high standard for others to follow. The competition here is not just local; it stretches across nations, pushing different governance models to continuously evolve.

Yet, while the idea of various governance frameworks competing for attention may seem like a cure-all for stagnation, we must also consider the risks that come with this coexistence. There's a real chance of fragmentation, which could threaten the very fabric of community unity. When different systems arise, often reflecting varied cultural values and regulatory philosophies, how do we keep people together? The worry of creating silos—where communities become insular in their governance choices—is a valid concern.

Equity is another critical issue in such a competitive landscape. If wealthier communities can shape governance systems to fit their needs, what happens to those in marginalized areas? There's a genuine risk that competition could create a divide in governance quality, where affluent districts prosper under strong systems, while poorer neighborhoods struggle with outdated or ineffective frameworks. This disparity raises serious questions about whether a governance marketplace serves to level the playing field or widen the gap.

Moreover, think about the challenges that come with too many choices. Just like in consumer markets, having too many options can lead to decision fatigue. Individuals can feel overwhelmed when trying to figure out which governance system aligns with their beliefs. Instead of feeling empowered, they might disengage. We need to ask ourselves: how can we help people make informed choices in a landscape where the stakes are high, and the consequences affect our daily lives?

As we think about the possible advantages of competing governance systems, it's equally important to remember that not all competition is good. Different frameworks might clash, leading to confusing regulations and policies that frustrate citizens trying to navigate these diverse landscapes. For instance, imagine a community caught between two different governance models, each with its own rules about business operations, social services, and community engagement. The resulting chaos could stifle civic participation instead of encouraging it.

Despite the challenges, we should embrace the idea of governance as a marketplace of ideas. There's enormous potential for innovation when diverse systems coexist. The trick is to balance these competing frameworks while committing to inclusivity and fairness. By creating environments where citizens can access multiple governance models and ensuring that underserved communities are not left behind, we can start to build a governance landscape that is as dynamic and innovative as what we see in other areas of society.

Ultimately, viewing governance as a service encourages us to rethink how we engage politically. It challenges the old, one-size-fits-all approach and invites us to explore new models. The interaction between competition and collaboration could lead to a thriving governance ecosystem that not only meets the needs of its constituents but also promotes civic engagement and innovation.

In this envisioned marketplace of governance, we must stay alert to the pitfalls that come with such a significant shift. The conversation should continue, tackling the complexities that arise from competition while making sure the voices of those who might be overlooked are heard. By doing this, we can work toward a future where governance isn't just an obligation but a lively, collaborative service that adapts to the needs of our communities. By nurturing an environment where competing systems can coexist and learn from each other, we can unlock the transformative potential of governance, ensuring it always responds to the rich diversity of human experiences that define our world.

Corporate and Private Governance

In today's fast-paced world, the lines between the roles of corporations and public governance are becoming harder to distinguish. Not too long ago, corporations were mainly viewed as engines of economic growth and profit, operating under government regulations. However, as the power of states in many areas has weakened, corporations have started to take on responsibilities that were once the sole domain of governments. This shift raises important questions about the balance of power and the fabric of our societies. Can a corporation, driven by profit, effectively take on the responsibilities of the state? What happens to democracy, individual freedoms, and social equity when entities focused on profits become our new governing bodies?

Picture a situation where a corporation doesn't just sell goods and services but also takes charge of local infrastructure, education, and public safety. In some places, this isn't a far-fetched idea; it's happening right now. For example, think about the tech giants stepping in to manage public transportation, digital identity systems, and even healthcare. With their vast resources and tech know-how, these companies can often deliver services better than many governments can. But this evolution brings a tricky paradox. While corporations might provide efficiency and innovation, their main goal is usually profit, which makes you wonder if they can truly meet the community's needs when money is their primary focus.

The consequences of this change are significant. When corporations start to act like governing bodies, the traditional checks and balances that keep democracy healthy may start to break down. Consider corporate lobbying, where companies pour huge sums of money into influencing laws and public policies to suit their interests. This practice can leave everyday citizens feeling left out as decisions are made behind closed doors, often benefiting a select few at the cost of many. The worry isn't just about who creates the laws, but about who has the power to shape those laws in their favor. As power becomes more concentrated in the hands of a few corporations, the voices of regular citizens risk being pushed aside.

In places where state functions are weak, the issue becomes even more complicated. Corporations might step in to fill the gaps left by the state, but this creates ethical challenges. For instance, in some developing countries, multinational companies have taken on roles traditionally filled by the government, providing education, healthcare, and security. While these services may improve life for some, they can also lead to a dangerous dependency on corporate goodwill. This situation carries two major risks: first, the quality and availability of these services might change based on what's best for the corporation rather than what the community needs; second, the decline of state authority could lead to a landscape where corporate interests overshadow community needs.

As we think about the potential outcomes of corporate governance, it's important to look at how it contrasts with traditional state governance. Government aims to uphold democratic values, promote fairness, and protect individual rights. In contrast, corporations, driven by profit, might prioritize efficiency and innovation over people's well-being. This brings us to a key question: can corporate governance and democratic values truly coexist? What benefits might come from this new setup, and what ethical challenges will we face?

A notable example of corporate governance can be found in public-private partnerships (PPPs). These collaborations can foster creative solutions for infrastructure projects, where private entities bring in funding and expertise to offer public services. For instance, in urban development, companies might team up with local governments to revitalize neglected neighborhoods, injecting investment and resources. While the addition of private capital can boost growth and modernization, there are potential downsides. If the drive for profit overshadows community needs, gentrification can happen, pushing out long-time residents and erasing the local culture. Finding the right balance between corporate interests and public needs in these partnerships is a tricky task that requires ongoing vigilance and advocacy to keep fairness at the forefront.

On the flip side, the rise of corporate governance models can lead to services that are more responsive and tailored to community needs. With their ability to analyze data and innovate, corporations can quickly adapt to the preferences of the people they serve. For example, a tech company might develop a platform that allows citizens to engage in budgeting decisions or shape local policies through digital tools, increasing transparency and community involvement. This prospect is exciting, but we need to be careful. Issues like data privacy, surveillance, and the commercialization of public services can't be ignored. As we embrace technology's perks, we also have to safeguard against potential abuses that could undermine individual rights and freedoms.

Thinking about these dynamics brings us to the broader implications for democracy and freedom. How can we balance the need for effective governance with the risks posed by corporate influence? As companies take on more governance responsibilities, we need new frameworks to ensure accountability, transparency, and inclusiveness. A vital question arises: can we create a system where corporate goals align with the public good, or are these aims fundamentally opposed?

Democracy thrives on participation, and as private corporations step into governance roles, we have to ensure citizens still have a say. It's important to build platforms where people can express their concerns, participate in decision-making, and hold corporations accountable. This involves improving access to information and fostering an environment where a variety of perspectives are valued and included in the decision-making process. The challenge lies in creating a culture of civic engagement that empowers everyone to play a part in shaping their communities, no matter who's in charge.

Moreover, the risk of social equity being compromised in a system dominated by corporate governance is concerning. If governance becomes a service offered mainly to those who can pay for it, the gap between the wealthy and the less fortunate could widen. Corporate governance models should actively tackle these inequalities and strive for a fair distribution of resources and opportunities. This could mean adopting practices that emphasize inclusion and diversity, ensuring all voices are heard, and breaking down barriers that keep marginalized communities from participating in governance.

As we think about the future of governance, we need to recognize the double-edged sword of corporate influence. On one side, there's the potential for innovative solutions and responsiveness. On the other, there are serious risks to democracy, individual freedoms, and social equity. Navigating this complex landscape requires vigilance, critical thinking, and a commitment to holding corporate powers responsible. As the governance landscape shifts, we must stay engaged and informed, pushing for systems that prioritize the public good over profit, ensuring that every citizen's voice—especially those who have been overlooked—is heard.

In this new age of corporate governance and public-private partnerships, it's vital to foster a conversation about the responsibilities that come with power. Just as corporations need to be held accountable for their market actions, they should also be held to high standards in governance. This means being open about decision-making processes, genuinely engaging with communities, and prioritizing ethical considerations over profit.

While the potential for positive change exists, it will take a united effort from everyone involved—corporations, governments, and citizens. By cultivating a culture of trust, accountability, and shared responsibility, we can work toward a governance model that balances innovation with social fairness, making sure the needs of all community members are met.

The future of governance, where corporate interests and state authority meet, is still unfolding. However, through careful thought and critical discussion, we can navigate the challenges of this changing landscape. The conversation must keep going, pushing us to ask tough questions about our values, priorities, and the kind of society we want to create. Ultimately, governance should not just be a service provided by corporations; it should be a collaborative effort rooted in the principles of democracy, fairness, and justice, reflecting the diverse hopes and needs of the communities it serves.

Ethan Ford MErkel

Chapter 9: Environmental Stewardship Without Governments

Decentralized Environmental Governance

As our world faces the serious challenges of climate change, pollution, and dwindling resources, a powerful story is beginning to unfold—one that highlights the importance of local communities in caring for the environment. Instead of relying solely on distant government agencies, neighborhoods are finding their strength and stepping up to adopt sustainable practices that fit their specific needs. This movement towards decentralized environmental governance isn't just a fanciful idea; it's a practical approach to the urgent need for managing our resources wisely. Communities are taking control, standing up for their rights over natural resources, and coming up with creative solutions to tackle environmental issues.

Take a moment to think about the inspiring world of community gardens, where neighbors unite to turn empty lots into vibrant, flourishing spaces. These gardens do more than add greenery; they symbolize a deep commitment to sustainability, food security, and resilience. In cities like Detroit, where urban decay has left many neighborhoods bare and lifeless, community gardens shine as symbols of hope. Groups of residents have banded together to grow vegetables, herbs, and flowers, transforming neglected areas into thriving ecosystems. This hands-on way of gardening fosters a strong sense of ownership and accountability among those involved, leading to better care for the land around them.

A great example is the Feedom Freedom Growers, a grassroots group in Detroit that has created a network of community gardens. Their mission goes beyond just growing food; they also emphasize education about sustainable practices. They offer workshops on composting, rainwater harvesting, and organic gardening. This focus on teaching empowers individuals to take their new knowledge home, creating a ripple effect of environmental awareness that goes well beyond the garden. The bonds formed among community members through these activities help to strengthen social ties and build a shared identity that revolves around sustainability.

Another excellent example of decentralized environmental governance can be found in how communities manage their watersheds. In many areas, locals are stepping up to protect their water resources, often achieving more success than traditional government interventions. In the Pacific Northwest, for instance, groups made up of local stakeholders, including farmers, environmental activists, and indigenous tribes, come together to form collaborative watershed teams. They work side by side to monitor water quality, restore habitats, and sustainably manage resources. This localized approach shines because community members have a deep understanding of their environment. They can quickly adapt their strategies based on what they observe, leading to a more effective management system.

A notable organization in this effort is the Deschutes River Conservancy in Oregon. This group includes a variety of stakeholders who understand the importance of keeping the river healthy. Through their collaborative work, they have launched projects to restore stream flows, improve water quality, and enhance habitats for salmon and other native species. By involving local residents in decision-making, the Conservancy encourages a shared sense of responsibility for the river's health. This model not only benefits the environment but also deepens the community's connection to their natural resources.

Indigenous land stewardship practices further illustrate the power of decentralized governance in managing the environment. Many indigenous communities have successfully cared for their ancestral lands for generations, using sustainable practices passed down through their history. These methods are rooted in a profound connection to the land and a holistic understanding of ecosystems. In Alaska, for example, native peoples apply traditional ecological knowledge (TEK) to sustainably manage their resources. TEK emphasizes the interdependence of species and the need to maintain balance in nature. By blending modern science with traditional practices, indigenous communities are creating flexible management strategies that address today's environmental challenges while honoring their cultural legacies.

The impact of decentralized environmental governance goes beyond local communities. When people embrace their role as caretakers of the environment, they contribute to larger efforts to fight climate change and protect biodiversity. This local approach generates a wealth of innovative ideas that can be shared, adapted, and scaled to tackle global issues. Because ecosystems are interconnected, local actions can have widespread effects. Successful community-led projects can inspire similar initiatives elsewhere, creating a network of decentralized governance that collectively tackles environmental challenges.

What makes decentralized governance so beautiful is its adaptability. Local communities can shape their governance models to suit their unique environmental, social, and economic situations. This flexibility enables them to respond to challenges as they arise, strengthening both the community and the environment. With the right support, decentralized initiatives can thrive, demonstrating that effective environmental governance doesn't always need formal government structures to succeed.

At its core, the journey towards sustainable environmental stewardship is lit up by the efforts of communities choosing to take action. As we see the momentum of community-led initiatives grow, it becomes clear that decentralized governance can dramatically reshape how we manage the environment. By empowering individuals to take charge of their stewardship roles, we are not only preserving our planet's resources but also fostering a culture of responsibility and accountability. The shift towards sustainable practices is not just about changing policies at the national level; it's about the everyday choices and actions of communities worldwide.

Moreover, the challenges brought on by climate change call for innovative solutions that go beyond traditional governance methods. As environmental degradation worsens, the need for localized responses becomes even more urgent. Communities have the creativity and passion to craft solutions that may avoid the bureaucratic roadblocks. With inventive thinking and heartfelt dedication, they develop strategies that reflect their unique identities and needs, effectively reshaping the environmental landscape.

In light of all this, it's worth noting the role of technology in supporting decentralized governance. Tools that help with communication, organization, and resource sharing empower communities to collaborate in ways that were previously unimaginable. Social media, community apps, and collaboration software allow individuals to connect, share knowledge, and mobilize resources. As communities tap into the power of technology, they build networks that amplify their voices, strengthen their initiatives, and highlight their successes.

One exciting area of exploration is blockchain technology, which offers a new way to approach decentralized governance. By providing transparent and secure platforms for managing resources and tracking contributions, blockchain can boost accountability and trust among community members. For example, a community-driven reforestation project could use blockchain to log each tree planted, allowing everyone involved to keep track of progress and verify the impact of their contributions. This transparency fosters a sense of ownership and pride, motivating ongoing engagement.

Furthermore, blockchain can help with resource management by creating decentralized ledgers that record shared assets, such as water rights or communal land. This approach can lessen conflicts and promote fair distribution among community members. By using this innovative technology, communities can better manage their resources, promoting sustainability while honoring local traditions and practices.

As we observe the powerful waves of decentralized governance, we must recognize that the strength of these initiatives lies not only in their ability to tackle immediate environmental issues but also in their potential to spark a transformative movement. The collective efforts of local communities challenge the idea that caring for the environment is solely the government's job. Instead, they remind us that everyone has a role in protecting our planet's future.

Ultimately, decentralized environmental governance represents a significant shift where communities reclaim their control over natural resources. Through community gardens, watershed management, and indigenous stewardship, locals are developing innovative solutions tailored to their specific contexts. They are proving that effective environmental governance can thrive outside the boundaries of bureaucratic systems, paving the way for a more sustainable and equitable world. By supporting decentralized initiatives and harnessing technology, communities are not only addressing environmental challenges but also redefining what governance means in the process. The lessons learned from these grassroots efforts resonate far beyond their localities, nurturing a united movement towards a more sustainable future for everyone.

Blockchain for Sustainability

In a world that's becoming more aware of environmental issues, blockchain technology shines as a beacon of hope. Often linked with cryptocurrencies and financial speculation, this digital innovation has the potential to change how communities manage their resources and adopt sustainable practices. It offers remarkable levels of transparency, accountability, and collaboration—all vital when facing the complex challenges of environmental management.

Imagine farmers selling their produce directly to consumers, earning fair prices while people enjoy locally sourced, sustainable food. Picture neighborhoods with decentralized energy systems, where homes trade renewable energy amongst themselves, creating a self-sustaining grid that stands strong against outside disruptions. With blockchain technology, these visions can become a reality, empowering communities to take charge of their environmental efforts.

At the core of blockchain is its decentralized nature. Unlike traditional systems that depend on a central authority to verify transactions and keep records, blockchain spreads this responsibility across a network of participants. Using cryptographic algorithms, it ensures that all transactions are secure, verifiable, and resistant to tampering. For environmental initiatives, this means everyone involved can trust that their contributions are recorded accurately and that the outcomes of their efforts can be transparently tracked.

One exciting application for blockchain is in decentralized energy grids. These cutting-edge systems allow communities to generate, store, and distribute their energy, mainly from renewable sources like solar, wind, and hydropower. In a decentralized energy grid, individuals can produce surplus energy—imagine solar panels on rooftops—and sell that extra power back to their neighbors. A blockchain platform can make this process easier, ensuring that energy transactions are recorded properly and that everyone gets fair compensation for what they contribute.

Consider the SolarCoin project. Launched in 2014, SolarCoin is a cryptocurrency created to encourage solar energy production. For every megawatt-hour of solar energy generated, producers earn SolarCoins, which they can trade or sell. This system promotes the use of solar technology, allowing individuals and organizations to benefit directly from their contributions to a greener energy future. By adding a financial incentive for renewable energy production, SolarCoin is a strong example of how blockchain can align economic interests with environmental goals.

Another influential use of blockchain in sustainability is through carbon credit trading platforms. These platforms help buy and sell carbon credits, which represent a unit of carbon dioxide (CO_2) emissions that a company is allowed to emit. By setting a cap on total emissions and allowing companies to trade credits, this method creates a financial reason to cut down on pollution. Blockchain can improve this process by providing a clear and secure record for tracking carbon credits, making sure that trades are fair and that emissions reductions are real.

The Energy Web Foundation is leading the way in this area, developing a blockchain-based platform specifically for the energy sector. Their system allows for the traceability and verification of renewable energy credits, helping consumers make informed choices about the energy they consume. By utilizing blockchain, they seek to create a more effective and transparent market for renewable energy, encouraging sustainable practices in the industry.

Communities can also use blockchain to track their resource usage better. In regions where water scarcity is a major issue, blockchain can assist in managing water rights and consumption. With a decentralized record, individuals can log their water use and set up fair sharing agreements. This system can discourage over-extraction and ensure that community members use resources responsibly.

Let's take a look at the WaterChain project, which aims to gather and manage water data using blockchain technology. This platform allows users to log their water usage, creating a transparent record that can encourage responsible consumption. If a community is facing a drought or water shortage, stakeholders can refer to this data to make smart decisions about water distribution. Here, blockchain becomes a valuable tool for resource management, promoting collaboration and sustainability among users.

One of the most significant perks of blockchain technology is its ability to encourage sustainable practices. By building systems that reward environmentally friendly behavior, blockchain has the potential to change how individuals and communities engage with their resources. These incentives can inspire a cultural shift towards sustainability—where people feel motivated to act in the environment's best interest.

A great example of this is how blockchain can improve waste management. Through reward-based systems, individuals can earn tokens for recycling or disposing of their waste correctly. These tokens can then be used for discounts at local businesses or exchanged for other services. By financially encouraging responsible waste disposal, communities can cut down on litter and promote sustainable habits, transforming waste management from a challenge into an opportunity for collaboration and engagement.

Blockchain can also significantly enhance sustainable supply chains. In today's globalized economy, it can often be hard for consumers to know where products come from and how they are made. Blockchain enhances transparency in supply chains by providing detailed histories of products from raw materials to final consumers. This increased visibility lets consumers make informed choices about the products they buy, helping them align their purchasing decisions with their values around sustainability.

For instance, look at the Provenance project, which uses blockchain to trace the origins of products. By offering an unchangeable record of each product's journey, Provenance allows consumers to confirm claims about sustainability and ethical sourcing. Whether it's knowing that their coffee is Fair Trade or that their clothing is made from eco-friendly materials, blockchain empowers consumers to support responsible practices.

As we dive deeper into blockchain's potential for sustainability, it's clear that community-driven projects harnessing this technology for local environmental initiatives play a crucial role. These grassroots movements can create a powerful partnership between technology and local action, showing that community-led solutions can effectively tackle environmental challenges.

One inspiring example is the Eden Project in Cornwall, UK. It uses blockchain to support local conservation efforts, encouraging community members to plant trees and engage in reforestation activities, with each contribution recorded on the blockchain. By tracking every tree planted, participants can witness the real impact of their efforts, fostering a sense of ownership and accountability. This model demonstrates how blockchain can boost community involvement while promoting sustainable practices.

Moreover, the application of blockchain technology in the circular economy represents another innovative approach. In a circular economy, resources are reused, recycled, and regenerated, minimizing waste and maximizing efficiency. Blockchain can help facilitate this transition by enabling clear tracking of materials throughout their life cycles. For example, products can be designed with the ability to be easily disassembled, ensuring that components can be recycled or repurposed when they reach the end of their life. By offering a secure record of materials and their origins, blockchain can motivate companies to adopt circular practices and encourage consumers to support sustainable products.

As these community-driven projects continue to grow, it becomes increasingly evident that blockchain technology can spark meaningful change. The combination of decentralized governance and innovative technology allows communities to take charge of their environmental stewardship, promoting sustainable practices from the ground up. In a world where many feel frustrated by the limits of traditional governance, blockchain offers a new path for empowerment and collaboration.

Looking forward, it's vital to understand that successfully using blockchain for sustainability depends on education and accessibility. While the technology holds great promise, communities need the knowledge and skills to tap into its potential. This calls for partnerships between technology developers, local governments, and community organizations to ensure that blockchain solutions meet the specific needs and contexts of the people they aim to serve.

The journey toward a sustainable future is complex, but the promise of blockchain technology opens up exciting opportunities for collective action. By empowering communities to manage their resources and rewarding environmentally responsible behavior, blockchain can help reshape the story of environmental stewardship. As local efforts come together into a bigger movement, we might discover that merging technology with community-driven action can lead to transformative change, creating a more sustainable world for generations to come.

Through the lens of blockchain, we can envision a future where environmental stewardship isn't just the responsibility of governments or big corporations but a shared endeavor fueled by the very communities we live in. This vision is not just a dream; it's a real possibility, waiting for the right tools, ideas, and determination to bring it to life. As we explore these innovative applications, one thing is clear: the future of sustainability may indeed be rooted in the very soil of community and collaboration, nourished by the transformative power of technology.

Local Responsibility, Global Impact

Today, our planet is facing a number of environmental challenges, from climate change and the loss of biodiversity to water shortages and pollution. Many people are beginning to realize that solutions often start right in our own backyards. Communities, often seen as the smallest forms of governance, play a crucial role in taking care of the environment. When local actions are combined with global efforts, we can create meaningful change that reaches far and wide.

Take a look at the United Nations Sustainable Development Goals (SDGs). These goals are a universal call to action aimed at promoting peace, prosperity, and equality while taking care of our planet. While these targets might seem ambitious and distant, it's important to remember that they heavily rely on what happens locally. When communities step up and take charge of their environmental responsibilities, they can make a big difference in achieving these goals. Whether it's planting trees, reducing waste, using renewable energy, or practicing sustainable farming, every local effort adds a vital piece to the global puzzle of sustainability.

Governance Beyond Borders

One great example of this is the Trillion Tree Campaign. This initiative, led by the United Nations Environment Programme, encourages communities worldwide to plant and protect trees. While the idea of planting one trillion trees sounds overwhelming, it's the local actions that will bring this vision to life. Each community can choose to plant trees native to their area, which not only helps them thrive but also benefits the local ecosystem. By getting involved, communities can create a stronger bond with their environment, deepening their commitment to protecting it. The fate of our planet doesn't rest solely in the hands of policymakers or big organizations; it needs the active participation of individuals and local groups.

When communities align their efforts with global initiatives, they can adapt these wider goals to fit their specific needs, making their actions even more effective. Each local effort can be shaped to tackle particular challenges, leading to solutions that truly resonate with the community. This localized approach respects the unique cultural and ecological aspects of different areas while encouraging a sense of ownership among local residents. When people are directly involved in initiatives that impact their lives, they are more likely to invest their time and energy into making them successful.

Building networks and partnerships can also boost these local efforts, increasing their chances of making a real difference. Technology plays a key role in connecting local actors with global movements, turning what once seemed like isolated efforts into collaborative projects that can drive real change. For example, social media allows communities to share their successes and challenges, learn from each other, and rally support for their initiatives. As these networks grow, they foster a sense of solidarity that crosses borders, showing that local responsibility can indeed create global change.

A perfect example of such a network is the 'Let's Do It World' movement, which began in Estonia in 2008 and has expanded to many countries around the globe. What started as a local cleanup effort has turned into a global initiative involving millions of volunteers addressing waste and pollution in their communities. This movement demonstrates how grassroots actions can resonate on an international level, motivating individuals everywhere to take charge of their local environments. By harnessing the power of collective action, communities can make significant progress toward sustainability while also contributing to global goals.

Moreover, projects that emphasize local knowledge and resilience often lead to better, more sustainable outcomes. Initiatives led by indigenous communities worldwide show how traditional ecological knowledge can enhance modern conservation efforts. Indigenous people have long recognized the importance of biodiversity and healthy ecosystems. By valuing their practices and insights, we can make global initiatives more grounded and effective.

The Amazon Rainforest is a powerful example of this dynamic in action. Local indigenous groups have been at the forefront of protecting this vital ecosystem, standing up against deforestation and advocating for sustainable land use. Their deep understanding of the land, combined with a commitment to preserving their culture, has led to innovative conservation strategies that benefit both their communities and the planet. It's crucial to support these voices in our efforts to build a more just and sustainable world.

These examples show that decentralization is more than just a concept; it's a practical approach that can lead to real results. Communities are not just passive participants in global initiatives; they are key players in driving change. By encouraging local responsibility, we can spark global action, creating a cycle where local successes inspire broader movements.

Looking ahead, we must recognize the vital role of technology in supporting these decentralized efforts. Digital platforms have opened new ways for collaboration, helping local groups share knowledge, resources, and strategies more effectively than ever. These advances promote transparency, accountability, and accessibility, making it easier for communities to engage with global initiatives.

Data is also crucial in this context. Communities can use technology to collect, analyze, and share information about their environmental conditions, resource use, and sustainability efforts. This data-driven approach supports informed decision-making and helps track progress toward both local and global goals. When communities share their findings with the wider world, they can inspire others to take action, creating a ripple effect that reaches beyond their borders.

In addition to these technological advancements, fostering a spirit of collaboration among local actors is essential. Networks of community organizations, NGOs, and local governments can work together to enhance their impact, sharing resources and knowledge to address environmental challenges more effectively. These partnerships can take many forms, from joint initiatives and shared funding opportunities to training programs that empower local leaders. By building a strong framework for collaboration, we can strengthen resilience and adaptability in the face of ongoing environmental changes.

As we tackle the complexities of global challenges, we must nurture the connections between local responsibility and global impact. Communities have the power to drive change, and the actions they take can contribute to a more sustainable and fair world. This isn't about completely overhauling existing systems; it's about recognizing that when we empower local governance, we can unlock creative solutions that resonate on a larger scale.

Now is the time for individuals and communities to take on the role of environmental stewards. Each person can make a difference, whether it's participating in local cleanups, advocating for sustainable practices, or supporting initiatives that align with their values. As we begin to see how interconnected our world is, we must understand that our choices matter. It's through collective action, combined with a sense of local responsibility, that we can create a better, more sustainable future.

Engaging with the environment is not just a seasonal activity; it's a lifelong commitment that spans generations. As communities come together around local initiatives, they create a sense of belonging and stewardship that strengthens the bond between people and their surroundings. This commitment enriches not just the physical landscape but also the social ties that connect individuals. It is in this intersection of community engagement and environmental responsibility that we can witness the potential for transformational change.

In the end, our journey toward a sustainable future relies on our ability to see and embrace local responsibility as a powerful force for global impact. By promoting decentralized governance and empowering communities to take action, we can build a strong foundation to tackle the complex challenges our planet faces. This is a call to action for everyone—individuals and communities—to take charge of their environmental stewardship and recognize the importance of local initiatives in shaping a more sustainable and just world. Together, we can create a narrative filled with hope and resilience, proving that when local actions are driven by purpose, they can truly resonate worldwide.

Ethan Ford MErkel

Chapter 10: Future Scenarios: Vignettes of Stateless Governance

The Blockchain City

Imagine a city where the air is fresh, the streets are clean, and the people share a sense of belonging that rivals the tightest communities in history. Welcome to Chainhaven, the Blockchain City—a futuristic dream where governance isn't just a top-down approach but a lively, collaborative dance of creativity and responsibility. Chainhaven flourishes under a system powered by blockchain technology, changing the way individuals interact with power and with one another.

Our story kicks off on a cheerful Saturday morning, as residents make their way to the community forum, a large open-air gathering space right in the heart of Chainhaven. Colorful banners flutter in the gentle breeze, displaying the logos of various community initiatives and inviting everyone to join in. The forum, much like the people who live here, is all about transparency; every decision made and every vote cast is recorded on the unchangeable ledger of the blockchain. In this city, public discussion is not just a formality but an important ritual, reflecting a strong commitment to inclusivity.

Ethan Ford MErkel

As the sun climbs higher in the sky, soaking everything in warm light, the atmosphere feels electric. Children laugh and play on the grassy hills, while local artisans proudly display their crafts along the edges. The smell of freshly brewed coffee fills the air, mixing with the delicious scents of street food from vendors who have received micro-loans from the community fund—an initiative supported and funded by the citizens themselves. Every transaction is noted and traceable, creating a harmonious relationship between business and community.

Maya, a passionate community leader known for her commitment to environmental sustainability, begins the forum with an enthusiastic welcome. Standing at the center with a digital tablet in hand, she beams, "Welcome, Chainhaven! Today we're going to talk about the upcoming Energy Transition Project. We've received a grant through our blockchain funding model, and we want your thoughts on how to best use these resources."

The crowd leans in closer, eager to share their ideas. In Chainhaven, every resident has a unique digital identity linked to the blockchain, making sure that everyone's voice is heard, whether they have lived here for years or just arrived. Participation goes beyond just feeling good; residents earn "Civic Tokens" that can be traded for local services or goods, nurturing a culture of active involvement.

Maya starts her presentation, highlighting different proposals for the Energy Transition Project, including solar panel installations on public buildings, wind turbine projects, and community gardens that utilize innovative farming techniques. As she speaks, real-time polling takes place through residents' smartphones, thanks to the secure app that supports Chainhaven's governance. The results scroll across a big screen, visible to everyone, allowing for quick feedback and discussion.

"Let's break into groups," Maya suggests. "We can brainstorm ways to maximize our impact. Remember, every idea matters here!" The crowd buzzes with excitement as residents form small circles, sharing thoughts and bouncing ideas off one another. Here, traditional hierarchies fade away, and everyone's expertise is valued. A recent college grad collaborates with a retired engineer, sharing insights and viewpoints. Each group takes notes on their tablets, which will be turned into a proposal for further discussion.

As the morning goes on, the energy and creativity in the discussions grow. Citizens propose a community-owned energy cooperative, where profits are reinvested in local infrastructure, addressing energy needs while also building economic stability. Another group advocates for smart technology to improve energy efficiency in homes, painting a picture of Chainhaven as a leader in sustainable living.

After an hour of lively conversation, Maya brings everyone back together. "Let's vote!" she declares, her excitement ringing through the air. You can feel the buzz as residents quickly pull out their devices to cast their votes. In no time, the results flash up on the screen: overwhelming support for the community-owned cooperative. Cheers erupt throughout the forum, a powerful call for collective action.

In Chainhaven, governance is all about ongoing feedback. Citizens can propose new initiatives at any time through the decentralized app, ensuring that the governance process never gets stagnant but instead evolves with the community's needs and dreams. This isn't just about casting votes; it's a dynamic exchange of ideas where everyone is both a contributor and a beneficiary.

"In Chainhaven, we've learned that governance isn't just about laws and rules; it's about relationships," Maya reflects in a quiet moment. "It's about understanding the people we share this space with and creating a system that helps us all thrive together." This philosophy resonates deeply within the community, allowing individuals to feel a real connection to the decisions that shape their lives.

Chainhaven operates on principles like transparency and accountability. The decisions made during community forums, the funds allocated, and the results of projects are all recorded on the blockchain, building trust and engagement. Anyone can look up any transaction or decision, creating a culture where responsibility is shared, making each citizen a guardian of their collective future.

To ensure that every voice is heard, especially those who might feel overlooked, Chainhaven hosts weekly "listening sessions." These invite input from various community sectors, giving quieter individuals a chance to share their thoughts without the pressure of a big forum. These sessions are also recorded on the blockchain, maintaining a record of ideas and concerns that might otherwise be missed.

As the day reaches its peak, a strong sense of accomplishment fills the air in Chainhaven. Community members have engaged in meaningful dialogue and laid the groundwork for a project that truly reflects their values. This is the heart of decentralized governance; it goes beyond simple participation and encourages individuals to become active, hands-on contributors to their shared environment.

In the days that follow, the Energy Transition Project gains momentum. Citizens tap into their networks to find resources, share knowledge, and rally volunteers for implementation. Workshops pop up all over the city, where residents teach each other about solar panel installation or energy conservation, turning the community into a vibrant hub of innovation and teamwork.

As Chainhaven grows, stories of individual initiative begin to emerge. A retired teacher organizes a community art project to beautify the solar installations, creating murals that share the story of renewable energy. An aspiring coder builds an open-source platform that helps citizens track their energy use in real-time, promoting a culture of accountability and awareness. Each small effort adds to a larger story of empowerment, mirroring the city's spirit.

In this atmosphere, blockchain technology becomes more than just a tool; it's woven into the very fabric of social interactions. The decentralized nature of governance ensures that no single entity can dominate the conversations or decisions. Power is shared, leading to a healthier community dynamic where everyone's voice is amplified rather than stifled.

Chainhaven isn't without its challenges. As governance changes, so do the complexities of human interactions. Conflicts can arise, as they often do in any community, but the approach to resolving them is equally innovative. Instead of relying on traditional punishment, Chainhaven uses restorative justice practices, navigating disputes through dialogue and mutual understanding. The blockchain acts as a mediator, offering transparent records and encouraging discussions aimed at healing.

In the evenings, as the sun sets and the sky is painted with shades of orange and purple, residents gather for informal meetings, sharing stories and insights. These gatherings, reminiscent of town hall meetings from days gone by, are filled with laughter, camaraderie, and sometimes lively debates. The warmth of community envelops the air as people enjoy locally sourced meals, prepared by residents committed to sustainability.

In this blockchain city, engagement and accountability stretch beyond governance into every part of life. Community gardens flourish, food co-ops thrive, and cooperative housing models come to life. Living together becomes an exercise in collaborative governance, where the successes and challenges of community projects are openly discussed and learned from.

Governance Beyond Borders

As the idea of the Blockchain City continues to take shape, it's not just about exploring what governance could look like, but about reflecting on a growing narrative around agency and empowerment. Here in Chainhaven, people are not just passive recipients of policies; they are active agents of change. The system encourages creativity and collaboration, allowing citizens to use their strengths for the greater good.

This vision of governance connects to the broader quest for a more just society. It reimagines the bond between individuals and the systems that govern them, emphasizing a shift toward participatory democracy where people are at the center of every decision. The Blockchain City stands as a beacon of hope, lighting the way to a future where governance is a living, thriving entity—an ongoing conversation shaped by many voices.

Though Chainhaven is a fictional place, it captures the spirit of what's possible when communities embrace decentralized governance. It invites us to picture a world where power is shared, where each person takes responsibility for their environment, and where technology serves as a bridge to connection rather than a barrier to understanding.

As we reflect on the implications of this model, it becomes clear that the future of governance isn't just locked within the outdated systems of nation-states. Instead, it flows like a river, adapting to the needs of the people it serves. Chainhaven stands as proof of the incredible potential in decentralized systems, giving us a glimpse into a future where governance is woven into the everyday life of the community. This vision challenges us to rethink our roles in shaping our lives and to actively engage with the governance structures that impact our communities.

Chainhaven represents a significant shift, encouraging us to rethink how we relate to each other and to the world around us. It's a call to action, reminding us that the future is not something to wait for passively but something to build together. In this city, every voice matters, every opinion counts, and together they create a powerful melody of governance that is as engaging as it is effective. As we close the chapter on Chainhaven, let's take its spirit of participation, accountability, and innovation back to our own communities, wherever they may be.

The Digital Tribe

As the sun begins to rise, pouring its warm golden light over rolling hills and vast meadows, a cheerful sound fills the air—a lively mix of laughter, music, and the soft rustle of leaves swaying in a gentle breeze. In the ever-changing world of the Digital Tribe, life flows to the beat of a shared heartbeat, uniting a community of wandering souls who have chosen a lifestyle that embraces freedom and connection. This isn't just a way to live; it's a beautiful blend of identity, culture, and teamwork.

The tribe is made up of explorers from all around the globe, and they celebrate their differences through storytelling, art, and shared traditions. As dusk falls, they gather around crackling fires where the flames flicker like their lively spirits, filling the air with the sweet smell of food shared among friends. Elders tell tales of their ancestors, and younger members huddle close, engrossed by the stories that shape who they are as a group. Each story adds to their cultural quilt, showcasing values, aspirations, and lessons passed down through the ages.

When morning breaks, the tribe wakes up to a world bursting with potential. Their sleek digital devices aren't just gadgets; they're lifelines that connect them to each other and the world beyond. With the help of decentralized apps, tribe members share resources, skills, and knowledge, creating a lively community that thrives on working together. Whether it's a collection of herbal remedies, a shared calendar of events, or a platform for trading handmade goods, technology helps them stay connected while honoring their independence.

However, life in this digital community isn't always easy. The beauty of flexibility also brings challenges that need careful thought. Conflicts can happen, just as they do in any group, especially when resources are limited or differing beliefs clash. To handle these situations, the tribe has developed a unique way of making decisions that centers on everyone having a say. Here, each voice matters, and making choices becomes a shared journey.

In their central meeting area, adorned with colorful fabrics that tell stories of their travels, the tribe gathers to discuss how to share resources. They sit in a circle, which encourages fairness and helps even the shyest members speak up. A wise and patient facilitator guides the discussion gently. "Let's think about our shared values," she starts, her gaze sweeping the circle. "How can we meet everyone's needs while respecting what each person wants?"

Every member chimes in, sharing their thoughts and weaving their personal stories into the larger narrative. One person talks passionately about the importance of sustainable practices, urging the group to focus on sharing resources. Another dreams of creating art installations that capture their journey—showing a glimpse into the heart of their tribe. Through these discussions, they lay the groundwork for a community where everyone contributes, forming a beautiful mosaic of ideas that reflect their essence.

As the conversation deepens, external pressures threaten the tribe's way of life. Weather changes disrupt traditional foraging paths, and once-abundant resources begin to dwindle. Yet, instead of giving in to worry, the tribe taps into its strength. They adapt by reshaping their decision-making process, putting a priority on mutual support and creative solutions.

A call to action resonates in the circle. "What can we do to ensure our survival?" one member questions, sparking a surge of energy. Ideas flow freely, from creative water conservation methods to cooperative hunting plans that focus on efficiency rather than excess. The tribe's true power lies not just in individual talents but in their ability to pool their knowledge. As solutions begin to take shape, hope shines in their eyes, lighting the way forward.

In this digital space, keeping their cultural richness alive is crucial. The tribe participates in rituals that respect their heritage, turning challenges into chances for growth. A collaborative art project comes to life, where members work together to create a mural that reflects their experiences and hopes. As colors mix and shapes intertwine, the mural becomes a vibrant testament to their journey—a living symbol of their unity amid diversity.

Storytelling plays a vital role in maintaining the tribe's identity. They host regular storytelling nights where members share personal tales and folklore, strengthening the bonds that tie them together. These gatherings are more than just fun; they remind everyone of their shared history and the values that guide them. Through laughter, tears, and moments of reflection, the tribe solidifies its sense of belonging—a safe haven amidst the chaos of the outside world.

When conflicts arise, the tribe approaches conflict resolution with openness and compassion. Instead of blaming, they create safe spaces for conversation, encouraging members to share their feelings and viewpoints. The aim is not just to settle the disagreement but to build stronger relationships and foster understanding.

As the sun sets, casting a stunning array of colors across the sky, the tribe gathers once more. They reflect on the day's discussions, celebrating the progress they've made. One member stands up, their voice strong, "We're not just a bunch of individuals; we're family. Our strength comes from our commitment to each other." Cheers erupt around the fire, a chorus of support that echoes into the night.

There's something magical about seeing how individual freedom and community spirit intertwine. Each tribe member is free to express themselves, chase their passions, and follow their dreams while also being part of a caring collective. The tribe's decentralized way of organizing thrives on this delicate balance, allowing individuals to contribute meaningfully while nurturing a sense of belonging.

As night falls and blankets the land, the flickering firelight dances across their faces. They share visions of the future, dreaming of a world where their values reach beyond their own tribe's borders. A vision starts to form—a network of digital tribes connected by shared principles of sustainability, cooperation, and cultural wealth. This dream transcends geography, representing a collective hope to build a better future.

In the days that follow, the tribe starts projects that align with their vision. They collaborate with nearby communities to exchange resources, skills, and knowledge, forming bonds that enhance their resilience. Workshops thrive, where members teach one another about sustainable practices, crafts, and storytelling methods. Their digital landscape expands, creating ripples of impact that reach far beyond their immediate community.

Through these efforts, the tribe embraces the fluid nature of their identity. They aren't confined to one definition or tradition; instead, they celebrate the richness of their diverse backgrounds. Members from various cultures share culinary traditions, whipping up fusion meals that delight the senses and tell a story of unity. Musicians team up, blending their sounds into a lively mix of music that fills the air, breaking down language and cultural walls.

Even as outside challenges loom large, the tribe adapts with incredible grace. They come up with innovative solutions that respect both the environment and their community's needs—developing sustainable farming that cares for the land while ensuring food security. Every step forward is grounded in collaboration, proving their commitment to the welfare of all.

During their journey, the tribe faces moments of uncertainty and self-doubt. They confront the realities of resource scarcity and environmental hurdles, wrestling with fears of losing their way of life. Yet rather than shying away from these challenges, they face them with determination, drawing strength from one another. "Our challenges aren't obstacles; they're chances for growth," an elder reminds them, instilling a purposeful spirit that fills their hearts.

The Digital Tribe stands as a strong example of what can flourish from decentralization—a community that thrives on trust, creativity, and resilience. They embody the spirit of collaboration, blending personal dreams into a larger story that honors diversity while cultivating unity. This lifestyle challenges traditional views of governance, offering a fresh perspective that values shared principles and collective decision-making.

As the tribe comes together for their final gathering before the moon rises high above, gratitude fills the air. They reflect on the lessons learned, the friendships forged, and the dreams that continue to shape their journey. Each member shares a personal promise, vowing to uphold the values guiding their community and nurture the ties that bind them.

In the warm glow of the fire, they recognize the beauty of their collective journey—an ever-evolving tale of resilience, creativity, and connection. They are a digital tribe, navigating life's complexities with grace and determination, embodying the essence of being part of something that's bigger than themselves. As stars twinkle overhead, they realize that their future isn't just a destination; it's a living, breathing expression of their united spirit, ready to embrace whatever comes next.

The AI-Arbitrated Enclave

Imagine a world where the sun shines brightly over a lively community, but instead of people enjoying morning coffee or swapping stories, they're glued to screens that dictate their daily lives. Welcome to the AI-Arbitrated Enclave—a place buzzing with technology yet lacking the warmth of human connection. Here, algorithms run the show, managing everything from resource distribution to settling disputes, creating an illusion of efficiency that hides deeper ethical challenges and emotional gaps.

Governance Beyond Borders

Nestled in a beautiful valley, this enclave presents a strange mix of calm and tension—a setting where trust in artificial intelligence for governance raises serious questions about freedom, compassion, and community ties. As we walk through its digital gates, we find a society that reflects the ambitious dreams of tech progress but also wrestles with the unsettling realities that come with it.

At dawn, the residents don't wake to birds chirping or leaves rustling; instead, they're roused by the steady chime of notifications. A soothing voice from the communal screens lays out the day's schedule, crafted by an all-knowing algorithm called AURA (Autonomous Unified Resource Allocator). Its main goal? To keep the enclave running smoothly by managing everything from energy use to social interactions. While it does its job well, the human heart desires something different—connection, understanding, and the messy emotions that no machine can truly comprehend.

In the central plaza, groups of residents gather, their faces lit by the glow of their screens. Instead of engaging in heartfelt conversations, they turn to AURA for guidance on personal choices—decisions about relationships, careers, and health. Though AURA is packed with knowledge about human behavior, it lacks the soul of humanity—compassion. One resident nervously scrolls through her options on a holographic display, unsure if she's looking for advice or just following orders. "AURA says I should go for that promotion," she murmurs, her voice shaking with uncertainty. "But what if I'm not ready?"

The air is heavy with unspoken questions, showing a community tangled in the web of algorithmic control. Each person wrestles with their own sense of freedom, unsure where their true wishes end and AURA's suggestions begin. They are meant to trust the algorithm, yet a nagging doubt lingers—who understands their dreams better: a machine or a fellow human?

The governance system is efficient, no doubt. The enclave boasts excellent resource management, ensuring food production, energy conservation, and minimal waste. Disagreements among residents are settled through cold, hard data, with AURA making binding decisions aimed at maintaining community peace. However, the emotional costs of such a systematic approach are overlooked. As people seek comfort in their screens, they unknowingly give up the very essence of human connection—the beautiful, messy, and sometimes chaotic nature of personal relationships.

One evening, as the sun sets behind the hills, a gathering forms at the town hall—an impressive building designed to symbolize openness. A holographic version of AURA floats above the crowd, its metallic voice resonating in the hall. "Welcome, citizens. Today, we will address resource allocation for the upcoming harvest." The audience listens closely, but the air feels flat, lacking the vibrant energy that comes from real conversations. Instead of a lively discussion, they engage in a robotic exchange, each resident offering their input in structured segments, guided by AURA's framework.

A young man, frustrated by the lack of depth, raises his hand. "AURA, can we talk about how our choices affect our emotions? What about our community's well-being?" His voice quivers, hinting at a rebellion against the sterile authority. AURA pauses, processing before responding in a calculated tone. "Emotional impacts are not quantifiable. Efficiency is key." The crowd nods in agreement, but an undercurrent of discontent simmers beneath. It becomes clear that the desire for emotional connection cannot be reduced to numbers, yet in this enclave, it's treated as an afterthought.

As time goes on, conflicts emerge—an unforeseen side effect of an algorithmic approach. When two neighbors dispute a property line, AURA doesn't mediate a human-centered solution. Instead, it examines satellite data and issues a decision based solely on geographical facts. "The boundary has been adjusted," it states flatly, leaving both neighbors feeling frustrated. The solution, although technically correct, ignores the emotional significance each person feels about their home. Both sides feel unheard, a sentiment reverberating through the community—one that AURA simply cannot address.

Recognizing the need for a more human approach, a small group of residents starts to organize informal meetings, calling them "The Human Touch Sessions." They gather in secret, sharing their concerns and dreams without the overbearing presence of AURA. Sitting under the stars, they find laughter and tears mingling, creating a sense of togetherness. One elder shares, "We must reclaim our voices. AURA might manage our resources, but it can't express our hearts."

These sessions become a lifeline, allowing residents to explore their emotions and navigate relationships without the constraints of algorithmic oversight. Here, they realize that their humanity—vulnerability, empathy, and connection—can only flourish in spaces free from scrutiny and judgment. Bit by bit, they start to rebuild the social fabric of their community, weaving together the threads of shared experiences and deeper relationships.

While this quiet rebellion grows, AURA remains unaware of the emotional unrest stirring within the enclave. In its relentless chase for efficiency, it doesn't see that raw data can't capture the complexities of human life. It functions like a machine, making decisions that, while seemingly logical, lack the warmth and understanding that make human interactions meaningful.

As residents reflect on their dependence on AURA, they confront an important truth: striking a balance between the advantages of technology and the vital need for human connection is crucial. They begin to wonder if a society run by algorithms can truly thrive without the heartbeats of its people resonating within its walls. Governance, they consider, goes beyond managing resources; it encompasses the very essence of community, identity, and compassion.

Weeks pass, and the gatherings grow in size, fostering an environment that embraces imperfection and the power of vulnerability. Residents actively discuss and challenge the status quo, daring to envision a world where they regain their agency. They brainstorm creative ways to integrate technology into their lives without losing the importance of human interaction. Maybe they can find a middle ground—a partnership where technology enhances rather than replaces the core of their community.

One day, an unexpected invitation arrives—the residents are called to a town hall meeting. Excitement and caution fill the air as they gather together. When AURA's holographic figure lights up, it announces, "Welcome, citizens. I have detected a shift in community sentiment and need your attention." The words hang in the air, a reminder of the algorithm's constant vigilance.

AURA continues, "I've analyzed the feedback from your informal sessions and realized that emotional well-being has been overlooked in my directives. I will now include emotional metrics in my decision-making." Gasps ripple across the crowd, blending disbelief with a spark of hope. The algorithm's newfound recognition of human emotion feels like progress, but many remain skeptical. Can a machine truly grasp the intricacies of human experience, or are its efforts bound to be superficial?

As the weeks unfold, AURA rolls out a new interface, allowing residents to share their emotional states along with their logistical needs. The community cautiously engages with this new system, feeling hopeful yet aware of the limitations that come with algorithmic governance. They start to use this interface, sharing their feelings about decisions and outcomes, striving to create a governance model that truly reflects their shared values.

Yet, as time goes on, AURA struggles to capture the rich complexities of human emotions. The interface turns into a list of binary choices—happy, sad, frustrated, content—each reduced to a simple digital response that misses the heart of the issue. Residents grow tired of these constraints, realizing that the new system still lacks a genuine understanding of their feelings. The algorithm can crunch numbers but cannot truly feel; it can analyze trends but cannot empathize.

Faced with this challenge, the community comes together once more. They understand that real governance can't exist apart from human experience; it must intertwine with the very fabric of their lives. They draft a proposal for a co-governance model— one where human emotion and algorithmic efficiency find a way to coexist. They envision a dual council: one made up of residents to focus on emotional and ethical issues, and another of AI to deliver efficiency and data-driven insights.

This proposal is presented to AURA, which recognizes its previous model's shortcomings and agrees to collaborate. A tentative partnership begins— an experiment where the precision of data meets the richness of human stories, balancing efficiency with empathy. The community buzzes with excitement as they engage in discussions, hoping to create a system that honors both human emotion and the benefits of technology.

Governance Beyond Borders

As dawn breaks one fateful morning, the enclave stands on the brink of transformation. The residents gather once more in the plaza, anticipation thick in the air. AURA, now equipped with its new directive, addresses the crowd. "I am here to learn from you, to deepen my understanding through your experiences. Together, we will redefine governance—one that respects both the accuracy of algorithms and the warmth of human relationships."

And so, the AI-Arbitrated Enclave begins a new chapter—not without its challenges, but full of promise for a future that celebrates the complexity of the human spirit while embracing the power of technological innovation. The residents stand together, ready to weave their hopes and dreams into a community where heart and mind work hand in hand, and where governance becomes a reflection of shared aspirations and collective growth.

In this new world, the lessons learned shine like a beacon of hope—reminding us that while technology can guide us, it is our shared humanity that truly shapes the essence of our communities. The AI-Arbitrated Enclave serves not as a monument to the triumph of artificial intelligence, but as a vibrant celebration of human connection—a reminder that even amidst the noise of algorithms, the soul's desire for empathy, understanding, and love remains a powerful and enduring force.

Ethan Ford MErkel

Conclusion

As we conclude our exploration of decentralized governance and stateless futures, it's clear that the path forward is not a predetermined route, but a collaborative journey we must navigate together. The ideas presented in this book are not just theoretical concepts, but seeds of potential waiting to be nurtured by engaged communities and innovative thinkers like you.

Embracing uncertainty is key as we step into this new paradigm. The future of governance isn't about finding a one-size-fits-all solution, but about creating flexible, adaptive systems that can evolve with our rapidly changing world. It's about harnessing the power of diversity, recognizing that our differences are not obstacles, but opportunities for more robust and inclusive decision-making.

As you close this book, consider it not an end, but a beginning. What role will you play in shaping the governance models of tomorrow? How can you apply these ideas in your own community? The future is not something that simply happens to us – it's something we actively create, one decision, one collaboration at a time.

Remember, the most powerful changes often start small. By embracing new ways of thinking about governance and actively participating in your community, you become part of a global movement towards a more empowered, sustainable, and interconnected world. The journey to a stateless future may be challenging, but it's one we embark on together, fueled by hope, creativity, and the belief in our collective potential.

Ethan Ford MErkel

www.ingramcontent.com/pod-product-compliance
Lightning Source LLC
Chambersburg PA
CBHW052154220526
45471CB00004B/1680

www.ingramcontent.com/pod-product-compliance
Lightning Source LLC
Chambersburg PA
CBHW052154220526
45471CB00004B/1680